# Tales From The Millinery Shop

By

David Charles Hart

 FriesenPress

Suite 300 - 990 Fort St
Victoria, BC, V8V 3K2
Canada

www.friesenpress.com

**Copyright © 2019 by David Hart**
First Edition — 2019

All rights reserved.

www.davidcharleshart.com

No part of this publication may be reproduced in any form, or by any means, electronic or mechanical, including photocopying, recording, or any information browsing, storage, or retrieval system, without permission in writing from FriesenPress.

ISBN
978-1-5255-5288-5 (Hardcover)
978-1-5255-5289-2 (Paperback)
978-1-5255-5290-8 (eBook)

1. History, Social History

Distributed to the trade by The Ingram Book Company

*To my father,*
Theodore Roosevelt Hart,
October 19, 1904 – February 17, 1981,

*And*

*To His Parents—*
an Interracial Couple from New York.

# TABLE OF CONTENTS

| | |
|---|---:|
| THE GRIMALKIN | 1 |
| LONG LIVE QUEEN SOTERIA | 5 |
| THE BEST ROMANCE I NEVER HAD | 29 |
| THE FACE IN THE LEAVES | 49 |
| THE MUSIC BOX | 79 |
| DISTORTIONS | 93 |
| THE NEREID NYMPH | 97 |
| THE ASCENSION | 115 |
| CHEERS | 133 |
| IMAGE REFERENCES | 137 |

"A woman's intuition is better than a man's. Nobody knows anything, really, you know, and a woman can guess a good deal nearer than a man."
— Mark Twain, The Gilded Age

## David Charles Hart

# THE GRIMALKIN

Gree-ins Dea' Rea-duh:

Guv-nuh, E'mm suh glad yeh 'cided 'uh pick up 'his book-n-read. I'd guess you'd call wha' E'mm sayin' is uh in-hrow-duck-shun. Buh' firs,' I should in-hrow-duce meself, I should. Muh name is Shȳne, uh Grimalkin, frum London in-nuh Uni-ed Kingdom, yeh know — England. E'mm more commonly called uh cat. E'mm owned by uh lady who's uh dress-maker. Her family name's Shȳne und-dey-r' known for 'heir dress-makin' brilliance. She began makin' dresses for duh toffs in duh 1800's and duh women who work in duh mill-nery shop follow her craf uh makin' fine dresses-n-hats. We lived in New York for a bi't, we did.

Now, yeh may ask jis' wha' kin" uh cat I yam? Well, I'm uh lille dif-feren' dan mos' cats, dem blokes. Yeh see, I kin talk. Fancy E'mm talkin' duh you righ' now in your head, righ'? You know, we cockney-English dun always speak our "t's" clearly. I'll try und improve as we go along. Enyways, I don' quite know 'ow muh human speech 'bility, wi 'his cock-ney-Bri-ish accen', came abou', buh I'm cer-n-ly nawt complainin'. Also, when I 'ear people talkin', I kin unner-stan' wha' 'hey be uh sayin', jus' like yeh kin unner-stan' me, in yer mind as you read, wha' E'mm sayin.'

'hese stories from duh women who work in a mill-nery shop in Uppuh-Stay' New York durin' duh early 1900's is qwite real, albeit wi' sum 'magination. Yeh 'magined 'hings, haven' yeh? Sure, yuh have. Yeh've had dreams tha' didn' make sense and you could nawt es-plain or unner-stand der meanin,' righ'? Like, yeh ever dreamed yeh uh runnin' 'way frum sum-one or sum-'hin'? Maybe yuh fell sum-one, or tha' sum-'hin' is

1

uh tryin' tuh kill yuh? Or maybe yuh had 'n ero'ic dream tuh fulfill sum sexual fan-uh-c? How 'bout eatin'? Yuh ever dream 'bout nosh?

Yuh know, I 'ad uh dream once. Yea, at's righ', a cat kin dream, ă-lease I know I did. I dreamed I's ow-side und hungry. Sudd'n-ly, I see 'his mouse dar-in' cross duh way, maybe 'bout nine me'ers frum where I am. I go runnin' afuh duh mouse. For sum reason, e - did'n' run tuh duh bushes und ... und hide frum me. Nor did-ĭ scamper up a tree tuh hide 'mong duh leaves. Mouse jus' keep runnin' in uh straigh' line.

Now, as E'mm gainin' on 'em, duh mouse sudd'n-ly stops, which cause me tuh stop for sum reason, probably frum be-n suh-prized. Buh-gi'-'his, duh mouse 'urns round duh face me, he's up on his hind legs, he is, und less-ow-uh loud squeal. Sudd'n-ly, E'mm encircled, I mean completely surroun-ed, by hundreds uh mice. Dey begins duh close in on me. Und yeh know wha' I do? Course, you don' know 'cause I haven' said. I wakes up!

I sez 'uh meself, I sez ... Blimey, I'll bloody be sick if 'n I le' 'hese li-uhle grey dus' balls wih legs scare me. I 'hen win—oww—n—caw' me uh mouse, bi' his bloody head off 'n spi' him in-nuh gudder, I did. I kicked duh ress' uv his mis-'bull ass in-nuh gudder also. Pard'n muh ruff language ear mate. I gi' carried 'way sum-'imes.

Enyways, back tuh duh s'ories. Dey're real-life experi'nces by 'hese women und 'heir families und friends. You'll read 'bout 'heir dreams und how 'hey lived 'heir lives. I'll be ow' your way, I will. You read. I'll be back much la-'er, I will, near end, wi' sumpin' I'll say. Maybe dur-in' las' couple s-'ories. Oh, pleez show sum luv for me friends who appear in a few s-'ories.

Las-'ly, Guv-nah, near yeh end, when yeh see 'his symbol uv meself — — you'll be uh knowin' E'mm speakin' so I b'lieve you'll fine 'hese s'ories inner-es-'in. I sure hope'n yeh do. Read-n-enjoy. Cheers!

*Louis and Louisa Gregory ~ circa 1911-1912 ~ New York*

# LONG LIVE QUEEN SOTERIA

"Sophie, you're late. You'd better hurry up and get to your work table. Madame Mittón will be here soon. And she expects to see all of us at our tables, and not just on our way there."

"Oh, shush, Mitzi. I'm arranging my things right now. Madame won't be upset. She knows how good a designer and creator of hats I am. Madame means owner, and she likes me."

"Ahh, vould ya lizen to zhe braggert now! Thinkin' she mighty high-minded, are ya now, Zophie?"

"Puh-leez, Annaliese. You know I'm just partially teasing. But I do think I'm among her best workers, after all. Don't you agree with me, Emma? Aren't I among the best here at making fine ladies' hats?"

"Umm, I—I guess so, Sophie. You do have a gift, so it seems, for this sort of thing. Uh-oh! Girls, I see through the window over here that Madame is coming. Look alive. You know the routine. We stand and greet her in unison as soon as she comes through the door."

"Good morning, Madame Mittón."

"Good morning, girls. Please, take your seats. I have some good news for you. I have here a good many orders from a large group of highly respectable ladies. They request that my shop—believing it to be the best millinery shop in Saratoga County—create and deliver a unique set of finely designed and highly fashionable ladies' hats. Each one wishes to wear their own exclusive, unique hat to the big derby in August. Let's see ... what day is today?"

"Madame Mittón."

"Yes, Mitzi."

"Today is Wednesday, May 19, 1897, Madame Mittón."

"Thank you for your specificity, Mitzi. That means we only have a little over two months, ladies, to showcase our talents. That could be a bit of a challenge, trying to accommodate so many women and their individuality, and—how should I say, eh?— *leur unicité*. Yes, Sophie."

"Excuse me, Madame Mittón, but I believe you have the best hatmakers for ladies in the entire state of New York. We can get it done."

"*Ja, wir sind die besten, Fräulein Mittón.*"

"Annaliese, please speak in plain English rather than German."

"Oh, zorree. Und, eh, I agree. Vee are zhe bezt."

"All right, that's the spirit I like to see! My shop does have a fine reputation to uphold. And I do believe I have the best hat designers that can be found anywhere. Here's what I want each of you to do."

* * * *

"Annaliese, leave your table and come over here for a minute."

"*Ja*, Zophie."

"I've got to keep my voice down. Remember last year when we made all those ladies' hats to be worn at the big horse racing derby, and we were able to scrape a few pennies together to attend?"

"*Ja*, zhure. I member, quvite vell."

"Well, I've been thinking about something ever since that day we went to the track. You know, it was a colored jockey who won that main event. And there were a lot of colored men riding those race horses that day."

"*Ja*, for zhure. I notize zem."

"I want to meet some of those colored boys, Annaliese. Will you come to the track with me this weekend?"

"*Scheisse! Du willst in schwierigkeiten geräten?*"

"Darn it, Annaliese! Puh-leez, speak English. What are you saying?"

"Eh, yu vant to get into trruh-bull?"

"Oh, no, Annaliese. We can keep it discreet, you know, sort of a secret. I just want to meet them, that's all."

"Are yu zhur? Oh vell, letz me zink about it, Zophie."

"Oh, c'mon, Annaliese, today is Wednesday and Saturday will be here before you know it. And judging from your conversations in the past, you seem to have a fondness for men, no matter what the color of their skin is. As long as they look handsome, you're okay with that, right? C'mon now, am I right?"

"*Ja*, Zophie, zat iz trrrue. I'm not, eh . . . eh, pree-ju-diz. If zuh man iz goot-lookin,' zen, vell, he'z juz goot-lookin.' Pay no mine to color; don't care 'bout zhat."

"Great! Then you'll go with me?"

"*Ja*, I'll go. Now, better getz back to your table before you getz into truu-bull. Ve must vurk on zeez hat ordurz."

"Oh, Annaliese, we're going to have such a good time this weekend! You just watch!"

\* \* \* \*

"Hey, you there, I want to ask you something. How did you learn to ride a horse so well?"

"Uhh, yuse talkin' tuh me?"

"Yes, I'm talking to you; and can you let that horse alone for just a minute? . . . Thank you. My name is Sophie, and this is my friend, Annaliese. We keep hearing from everybody about how great horse racing is—how it is so entertaining and thrilling! Why, I even read that horse racing is called the 'Sport of Kings.' So we went to the big derby last year, Annaliese and I, and we decided to take a Saturday off to come here. So, here we are. And you know what?"

"Naw, whut?"

"We admire how you colored jockeys ride so well, and . . . and there you go again! Can't you please stop fiddling with that animal and look my way for just a moment? . . . Thank you.

So, we decided to make our way down here to this track's stables and see if we could catch up with one or two of you colored boys. And looks like we have! So, tell me, where did you learn to ride like that?"

"Ma'am, I's . . . don't . . . thinks . . . weez should be . . . talkin' right now."

"And why not? We're not doing anything wrong?"

"C'mon, Zophie, ve should leave. Zis man iz buzy vith zat horze."

"Annaliese, I just want to know—"

"Hey, what are you two ladies doin' over here? Horace, what's goin' on? You know you shouldn't be talkin' with anyone, 'specially these two."

"Yas, suh, Mistuh Adam, suh. I wuz jus tellin' em—"

"Look, I got to get this horse into his next trainin' session before Mr. Wheelhouse gets back. Ladies, you'll have to pardon us."

"Just a minute, sir. My name is Sophie, and this is my friend, Annaliese. We came over from town to look into this horse racing business. And we just wanted to meet some of the boys that ride these horses and learn a little bit about the sport. That's all. We mean no harm and we sure don't want to get anyone, like Horace here, in trouble. But if I may ask before we go, who are you?"

"Beg pardon, ladies. Allow me to remove my hat. My name's Adam, Adam Hart. I'm the chief horse trainer for Mr. Thomas Wheelhouse, the owner of this here stable, and several of these horses. Uh, pardon me again. Horace!"

"Suh?"

"Go ahead an' take this horse over to the paddock. I'll be on directly."

"Yas, suh."

"Ladies, you best be leavin' here. This is not a good place to talk."

"Well, Mr.-Adam-Hart-The-Chief-Horse-Trainer, where is a good place and time we can talk? Annaliese and I would like to know more about, eh . . . um . . . race horses. Isn't that right, Annaliese?"

"Yez, zhure. Ve vant to know all about zim."

"Yea, I bet you do. All right, tell you what—and then you must go—you know where Gordon's Boardin' House is over at the west end of town, near where most of us colored folks live?"

"Not exactly, but I'm sure we can find it."

"Okay, good. Stop by any evenin', say after 7:00 pm. Ask for me. Miss Gordon is white, but she doesn't mind us colored folks minglin' with white folks like you in her place. You know, like in the drinkin' and eatin' area, as long as it's kept respectable. Know what I mean?"

"Yes, sure, I think I understand. We'll be in touch. You'll see us again. Thanks a lot."

"All right now; goodbye, ladies."

"Goodbye, Mr. Adam Hart."

"Yez, goot bye, Miztur Adam."

"Well, Annaliese, let's go home. But tell me, what do you think about those Negro fellows? Nice guys, Horace and Adam. Don't you agree? And wow, such good-looking dark-skinned men! What do you think, Annaliese? Annaliese?"

"*Mein Gott! Was für ein schöner schwarzer mann, dieser Adam. Sehr gut aussehend.*"

"Annaliese speak English! What are you saying? Annaliese? Annaliese!"

\* \* \* \*

"Good morning, Madame Mittón."

"Good morning, girls. Please, take your seats. I have some good news for you. Since Mr. Theodore Roosevelt won this year's 1898 election to become the governor of New York, I have tons of hat orders here for you. These are from ladies that want to sport the latest in unique, fashionable hats at the dances, balls, and various events celebrating his election."

"Madame Mittón?"

"Yes, Sophie."

"Before we get started on today's orders, if you don't mind, please tell us a little bit about Mr. Roosevelt's election victory for the governor's office. I've heard he is quite a—how shall I say? —an *adventuresome* man! And I even read somewhere that he had Negro soldiers, or cavalrymen I guess, that were part of his Rough Riders group during the Spanish-American War. Is that right? Colored men helped Governor Roosevelt during that war?"

"Yes, Sophie, that's right. I'm no expert, but I will tell you what little I know from what I've read, and from certain friends of mine who are involved in New York City's local and state politics."

"That would be great, Madame Mittón!"

"Yes, Sophie, I see by the nodding of everyone's heads that you are all in agreement. We can't spend too much time on this, and—uh, yes Annaliese, I see your hand. Go ahead, you can speak; but please, be brief."

"Madame Mittón, I'd like to know more about zee colored zoldierz zat helped Governor Roozevelt during zee war."

"Well, Annaliese, and for the rest of you, I can't say much about that because I really don't know. Here's what I've heard and read: Our governor reportedly showed great bravery when, on horseback, he led his men in the charge on San Juan Hill in Cuba. He fought other battles against the Spanish in Cuba, and supposedly, a regiment of colored troops helped him win some of those battles, Annaliese. A dear friend of mine in New York City said that Governor Roosevelt is a bit of an enigma, I'm afraid, when it comes to colored people. Sometimes he likes them, sometimes he doesn't, according to her. And she is colored. Anyway, she said that while Mr. Roosevelt was New York City's police commissioner, he cleaned up a lot of the corruption that plagued the city. So perhaps he'll do the same for our state, and maybe, just maybe, he'll do the same for our nation as president someday. We'll just have to wait and see. There, that's it, girls. Now let's get to work."

\* \* \* \*

"Well, Miss Sophie and Miss Annaliese, I really wasn't sure I'd see you two ladies again."

"I always keep my word, Mr. Adam Hart; that is, if I can. It was not difficult at all finding this boarding house. It's quite large, I see. A lot of, shall I say, different people mingle here."

"Yes, that's right, Miss Sophie. I always stay here durin' the horse racin' season because of Miss Gordon's open hospitality to anyone and everyone. It's a bit expensive to stay here but welcomin' to all. It's my home away from home."

"Oh, zo you're not frum 'round here, Adam?"

"No, Miss Annaliese, I'm from New York City, in a community called Queens. We recently were incorporated into Greater New York City."

"Zen how often you come up here to Zchuylerville? Und pleez, drop the Mizz. I'm Annalieze."

"All right, Annaliese. I generally get up here 'bout once a year, durin' the summer racin' season which lasts about four to five weeks. You see, I'm a trainer. I train horses to race. There are times I may come up in the spring, like now, here in 1899, and I may stay longer than the racin' season for any additional work with the horses I might need to do. I also do a lot of travelin' for my boss, Mr. Wheelhouse."

"My goodness, Mr. Adam. Whereabouts do you go to look for horses to train and race?"

"Oh, Miss Sophie, I travel all around the country—and even out of the country, as far down as South America—scoutin' and lookin' for potentially great race horses for Mr. Wheelhouse to purchase for his stables. Then I train them, hopin' to turn them into champion thoroughbreds and make us lots of money."

"My goodness, how exciting! Isn't it, Annaliese? Annaliese!"

"Miss Sophie, I think Annaliese is lookin' at me tryin' to figure me out. I'll just go over here to the counter and buy us some sarsaparilla sodas. I'll be right back."

"Annaliese? Annaliese, are you all right?"

*"Ich möchte mit diesem schönen schwarzen mann zusammen sein."*

"Annaliese, please! What are you saying?"

"I vant him, Zophie. I vant zat beautiful black man. I vant to hold him, zkveeze him! Und for him to zkveeze me—"

"Annaliese, what are you saying? Get hold of yourself!"

"*Nein*! I vant to let mezelf go, into hiz armz! Prezz my breazt againzt his naked, bare chezt. I don't know vhaz come over me, Zophie. Ever zince zhat firzt vizit, I can't get Adam out of my mind. Feeling haz been building ever zince. I vant him, Zophie."

"Annaliese, you barely know this man!"

"I don't care, Zophie. Adam haz touched my zoul. I can't explain, but he haz. I vant to zee him naked, und zen I vant him to put hiz vhite fluid inzide of me. Zophie, me . . . me female juz iz . . . Jesús, *meine Muschi is*t so *nass*!"

"Annaliese, I'm shocked at you! You don't know what you're saying, Annaliese! Annaliese, where are you going? Annaliese!"

*"Gott hilf mir. Ich bin so heß und geil auf diesen mann. Scheisse! Ich will, dass er mich die ganze Nacht fickt."*

\* \* \* \*

"Annaliese, where did you go?"

"Oh, Zophie, I vent to zee batzroom to, eh . . . eh, relief mezelf."

"Well, Adam brought us these sodas. He said he'll be right back. He went outside to talk with a couple men he said he needed to see."

"Zophie, zis Adam haz me head in a tizzy."

"Well, ladies, I came back to briefly greet you once again, and then I must be leavin'. I have some business I must attend to. There are a lot of things I have to get done to get through this racin' season and get ready for next year."

"Well, Mr. Adam Hart, Annaliese and I sure enjoy your company. And we'll come around from time to time, especially before we enter the new year—and the new century!"

"That's right, Miss Sophie, I forgot! The new year of 1900 is also the start of a new century!"

"Yes, Adam, the twentieth century will just be getting under way. And you know what else happens next year?"

"No, I don't. What else happens, Miss Sophie?"

"It is a presidential election year. And I suppose President McKinley will run for a second term in office. It's a shame a woman can't vote."

"Oh yes, I completely forgot about next year bein' an election year. And I agree with you. It's a shame women aren't able to vote. I expect that will change in the years ahead. Even most of us colored men either can't or don't vote, even though we now have the right to vote ever since Congress said we could, some thirty years ago."

"That's right, you can vote even though you're colored."

"Yes, and I do vote, Miss Sophie, in every election that I can. I do wish my favorite guy was runnin', though."

"Und who might zat be, Adam?"

"Theodore Roosevelt, the rough rider. That's my guy, Annaliese. I'd vote for him in a heartbeat."

"Vhy iz zat?"

"Because he cleaned up New York City from all the crooks, especially in the police department, when he was police superintendent. I can sleep better now at night."

"*Und ich möchte die ganze nacht mit dir schlafen, du schöner teufel-mann du.*"

"Uh, what did you say, Annaliese?"

"Nutzing, Adam. It vas nutzing important."

"Well ladies, I tell you what: I'll be leavin' for home in a few weeks. How 'bout you two come visit me in New York City next June, just before the start of racin' season. I'll show you around our great city. And I'll put you up in one of our fine hotels. How's that?"

"That's a lovely idea, Mr. Adam! I'm sure Annaliese and I would love to come see you, right, Annaliese?"

"Yez, to be zure. Love to come to zuh New York Zity."

"Great. Well, I best get goin', ladies. I look forward to seein' you again. So, take care of . . . oh my, Annaliese, you didn't have to kiss me on the cheek like that! I felt your tongue on my jaw; my-my-my."

"I vanted to. I vill zee you again, zoon."

"Annaliese!"

"It'z all right, Zophie, it'z all right. I love zhe tazte of dark chocolate."

"Uh . . . okaaay. Well. Bye, ladies. Till next time."

\* \* \* \*

"Hello, Miss Gordon. May I join you?"

"Of course, Adam. Please, have a seat. Business is pretty slow. I guess everyone is excited about the upcoming presidential election and reading all the newspaper articles about it. People are either in their rooms or with friends someplace, I guess. I suppose everyone is curious to know who President McKinley will pick as a running mate, since Vice President Hobart died last year. You going to the Republican Convention in Philadelphia next month?"

"No. But I do hope President McKinley will pick Mr. Rough Rider himself—Teddy Roosevelt. I really admire the guy. But even though I enjoy followin' politics, I need to get several horses ready to run. So, I'll just stay here in Schuylerville through May and June, go back and forth between here and the track, and then hit Saratoga Park in July. Then it's full steam ahead, and hopefully we'll rack up a few victories for Mr. Wheelhouse!"

"You really like your boss, Adam, that Mr. Wheelhouse?"

"Sure. I don't have a problem with him, Miss Gordon. He treats me good, pays me well. I get to travel, and at a time when a colored man like me is shown very little respect here in America. Mr. Wheelhouse does try—and I appreciate him for that."

"Well, you know we're only about thirty-five years removed from the Civil War, and racist feelings still run high. For sure in the south, but also right here in New York state."

"Oh, how well I know. Racial tensions are runnin' high back in New York City. And especially if people see a colored man with a white woman. They gotta be real careful, or someone is libel to put a bullet in a fella's back."

"Goodness, Adam, you believe things are that bad here in New York?"

"Absolutely, Miss Gordon. I tell all the young colored boys to watch their step around white women. I remember, just a few years ago, I had a side job workin' with horses at a stable over in Manhattan. There was this tall, rangy colored kid from Texas named Jack Johnson. He used to work with some of the horses, exercisin' them. He was quite a character, had kind of a wild way 'bout him. He used to shadow-box and spar with some of the other boys. And he talked about runnin' after white girls. I advised him to watch his step. Bein' with a white woman in the wrong place could get him killed."

"Interesting. What ever happened to him?"

"Last I heard, he was let go, I think for overworkin' the horses. He went back to Texas."

"Well, Adam, I sure hope he took your advice to heart and will stay out of trouble. And speaking of trouble, look who's walking in to see you—apparently, since she's walking straight over here. I'll leave you two alone! But remember, Adam: follow your own advice."

"Hello, Adam."

"Annaliese, what are you doin' here? It's almost ten o'clock at night. Where's your friend?"

* * * *

"Good morning, Madame Mittón."

"Good morning, girls. Please, take your seats. I have some good news for you today. As I think all of you know, this year, 1900, is a presidential election year, as well as the start of a new century. At last month's Republican Convention in Philadelphia, President McKinley chose our own Mr. Rough Rider himself, Theodore Roosevelt, as his running mate for Vice President. Yes, go right ahead and clap, that's fine. I'll join you. We can all clap for that."

"Madame Mittón?"

"Yes, Mitzi."

"Do you think Mr. Roosevelt may one day become president?"

"Quite possible, Mitzi, quite possible. But meantime, a very large group of Republican ladies from all over the state, and some from out-of-state, have placed orders with me in anticipation of another ball for President McKinley and his soon-to-be-Vice President, Theodore Roosevelt. Girls, I have literally *hundreds* of hat orders here! Being that we're in the latter part of July, I'll probably have to hire more help to get these hats out before November. And—yes, Sophie?"

"Sorry to interrupt you, Madame Mittón, but you may need to hire some replacement help to."

"Oh? Why is that, Sophie?"

"I visited with Emma yesterday, and she is very sick. Cholera, I think."

"Oh my, sorry to hear that. Emma is probably among those still affected by the last major outbreak from a few short years ago."

"Yes, ma'am. And also, I spoke briefly with Annaliese at her place last night, and she is not doing too well either. However, she did say that she would try to make it in a little later, probably by mid-day."

"All right. Thank you, Sophie. I see I'll have to get busy hiring a few new girls. But that's okay, we'll handle it, and we'll do a very fine job in the process and turn out exquisitely designed, fashionable ladies' hats. So, here's what I want you girls to do."

\* \* \* \*

"Hello, Zophie. Thankz for coming over. Come on in und have a zeet."

"Annaliese, I can't keep covering for you with Madame Mittón! You show up for a couple days, then you're gone for a day; then you show up for maybe a full week, and then you're gone again. I know you're seeing Adam, Annaliese. But you can't keep this up! You're missing too much work, and the gossip about you sleeping with a colored man is getting louder and louder!"

"Yea, Zophie, I know. Verd haz gotten back to me family, me dad und mum. Zay vill have nutzing to do vith me unlezz I ztop zeeing Adam, und I looze me inheritance. Zay are vealthy."

"Well, Annaliese, you have some tough choices here. You, my dear, are on the verge of losing your job at the millinery shop here in late August. And then to lose your relationship and inheritance from your wealthy family—over one colored man! We're a little behind in getting the hats out before election day in November, and—"

"Zophie, you're part right und part wrong. Yez, I could looze me job. Und yez, I could looze me mum und dad und zee money. But zee greater lozz iz if I looze me heart: Adam. I dearly love zis man, Zophie. Und I plan to marry him, und all zat goez vith it."

"What? Annaliese, are you serious? Have you lost your mind? I mean, I like colored guys too and want to be friends with them—maybe even sleep with one or two on occasion, you know, just for the fun. But we are white, Annaliese, as white as the driven snow! Adam, and others like him, are black, as black as the night. Black and white in a mixed marriage? Not good. White swans mate with other white swans. Crows mate with crows. That's just nature. Black and white just don't mix, at least not in the way you want to do it. Marriage? People will crucify you two. I mean, pardon my French, but damn!"

"It'z all right, Zophie. I don't need vealth, or popularity, or fine clothez, or itemz of luxury. I'll be happy und content with Adam und vhat little vee have."

"Annaliese, that all sounds good and noble. But is it reality? Horse racing season is pretty much over. When will you see Adam again?"

"He'z been in New York Zity for zee past few dayz. But I'll zee him zis evenin'. Zophie, I vant to zhare vith you a quote I learned back in

Germany vhile ztudying clazzic literature. It'z from zee Greek philozopher, Zocrates."

"Okay. Tell me, what is it?"

"*Das Geheimnis des Glücks liegt nicht darin, mehr zu suchen, sondern die Fähigkeit zu entwickeln, weniger zu genießen.* The zecret of happinezz iz not found in zeeking more, but in developing zee capazity to enjoy lezz."

"Well, Annaliese, if you marry Adam Hart, you better get used to enjoying a whole lot less, 'cause that's what you will have: a whole lot less. There is no place in America here in August 1900, that welcomes interracial marriage—nowhere and at no place. And that includes right here in the state of New York. Maybe one hundred years from now it will be different, acceptance of white and black being together. Maybe by then, the turn of a new century, color-blind love will be welcomed with open arms. But not today. Do you know that just for being together, you both could be killed by some half-crazed white racist? Do you understand that, Annaliese? Do you?"

\* \* \* \*

"Good morning, Madame Mittón."

"Good morning, girls. Please, take your seats. I have some good news and some not so good news for you today. I should say *sad* news, which I'll mention first. Our dear Emma Stone passed away last night from the cholera infection she's been fighting for some time now. Remember her grieving family, her husband—Paul, and her two little daughters—Emily and Emmelynn, and her parents ... I can't recall their names. Anyway, please pray for them all that they will find comfort in their hour of bereavement. Emma was a fine young woman, only thirty-two years old. We are very sad to lose Emma. She was a good hat maker. But life goes on, and so must the millinery shop. So, now for the good news: Let's try and put on a more cheerful face, as best we can, shall we? I want to introduce two new girls I've hired—will you two girls please stand? This is Rebecca, a very bright Jewish girl from Pennsylvania. She has an identical twin sister. And this is Lilly Ann, a twenty-something, sweet and pretty, colored creole girl from Louisiana. This is their first day, so please, let's take a few minutes and make them both feel welcomed to work here at the best millinery shop in the state. Afterwards, I'll give out your new work orders."

"Zophie, before ve greet zee new girlz, I need to talk to you for a minute. Let'z go over here to zeez little quiet corner."

"My goodness, Annaliese, what's wrong? You look so worried in the face. What's bothering you?"

"Zophie, two zings. I hear rumorz, talk, zat Emma, even zō, zhe had zee cholera, may not have died from it. Zay are zaying her death iz zuzpiciouz, Ja."

"Aw, shush, Annaliese. That's just wild talk. It don't mean anything."

"Maybe, Zophie, maybe. Az for me, I have not heard from Adam in weekz. He vent home for a few dayz at zee end of June, zen came up here for zha ztart of horze raczing zeazon. Zhen in early Auguzt, he vent back to New York. Before he left, he told me he vould be back zoon, even gave me zhe day. But here ve are at zee end of Auguzt, und I ztill have not heard from Adam, Zophie. I am zō vorried!"

"Annaliese, please don't cry. He'll show up, just you wait and see. Adam loves you just like you love him. C'mon, here's a handkerchief. Let's look cheerful, shall we? We've got to greet these two new girls. So, let's get up a smile, okay . . . okay? Ah yes, Annaliese, that's it, there's that lovely smile of yours! That's it! Let's go. Adam will turn up, I'm sure of it. And forget about them wild rumors regarding Emma's death. She died from cholera."

\* \* \* \*

"Peanuts, heaah! Git yo' red-hot roasted peanuts heaah! Peanuts, heaah! Git yo' red-hot roasted peanuts heaah!"

"C'mon, Junebug, c'mon, baby, run, run! You can catch the rest of the field. C'mon, c'mon, dammit! Pete, you're the goddamn jockey ridin' the blasted horse, use the whip. Use the whip, goddammit! C'mon, c'mon, use the . . . awww shit! Lost again! I give up. I train a horse to win at least one goddamn race, and he finishes near the back of the pack every time."

"Hey, mister, I can't help but overhear you talkin' out loud there to yourself. Your horse disappoints you?"

"*Disappoint* ain't a strong enough word for it. The nag is an absolute failure, and I trained that horse. The jockey didn't help none either. I'm sick over it. Me, Adam Hart, a first-class trainer of race horses who *win*. I mean, I *train* horses to win, not come in next to dead last like this nag always seems to do."

"Well, um, Adam, you can't win 'em all."

"Yea, but with this lazy-ass horse, I won't win anythin'. Not a damn thing. Oh well, to hell with it. Let me leave this goddamn Pimlico race track and get my black ass out of Baltimore and back to New York. You take care, mister."

\* \* \* \*

"Adam, vhere haf you been? I've been vurried zick! You don'z write or anyzing to let me know vhere you are. Und now here you are at me front door. Hold me, Adam, pleez. I mizz you, Adam. I mizz you zo much!"

"I know, Annaliese, and I'm sorry. I truly am sorry. Can you leave your place and go with me to get somethin' to eat? I'll tell you all about where I've been and what's been going on with me."

"*Ja*, zhure. Let me grab me coat und I'll be right zhere."

"Thanks for comin', Annaliese. Let's go someplace nearby that's within walkin' distance and where we won't have any problems eatin' there."

"Zat'z fine, Adam. I know juzt zee plaze, not too far from here."

"Great. Let's see, what is today's date?"

"It iz Friday, May 17, 1901."

"Thank you, Annaliese. You know, we've been datin' and spendin' nights together on and off for the past two or three years. I think it's high time we get married. Not today, but soon. And to hell with what people will say."

"Adam, I've been vaiting on *you*! I've been ready to marry you practically from zee firzt time I laid eyez on you!"

"Yea, I know. I just need a little more time. But let me tell you 'bout what's been happenin' with me from last year into this year."

"Zokay, I'm all earz."

"Last June, I was in the city to oversee the arrival of some horses, only about three or four, who were comin' into New York by boat from

Europe. Real nice thoroughbreds that had potential, given their breedin'. The boat containin' the horses had docked over in New Jersey at the Hoboken Pier. Somehow, someway, a fire got started at that pier—and you know those piers and everythin' around them, they're all wooden: the docks, the buildin's, the storage areas, it's all wood."

"Zoundz like a rezipee for dizazter."

"That's right, Annaliese, and it *was* a disaster. With the wind kickin' up, the fire spread quickly all along that part of the waterfront. Everythin' was ablaze: the pier, buildin's, boats, everythin'. And what made matters worse, some barrels of oil and turpentine caught fire and exploded. It was a goddamn mess, a real tragedy. We lost the horses, and by the time the fire was under control, I think a couple hundred people or more had died. It was terrible, just terrible."

"My goodnezz, Adam, I am zo zorry to hear zat! Vell, at leazt you made it out zafely."

"Yea. But that's not all, Annaliese. Last summer was very tough for me. Besides the fire, later in August, a race riot broke out in the city. I'm not sure exactly how it started, but a police officer was stabbed to death by some colored guy. Well, shit, as you can imagine, that set things off. The coloreds and whites got to fightin' over in a district called the Tenderloin. A lot of Irish live there, but more and more colored people, primarily from the south, started movin' in. But it really didn't matter where any of us colored people were in the city; bricks, bottles, and all kinds of stuff were thrown at us. I got hit with some garbage, but no harm done. But anyway, with all that goin' on, it messed up my usual routine schedule for trainin' horses. Needless to say, I got some catchin' up to do."

"Vell, Adam, like I zaid before, you made it out okay, und now you can begin anew. Your favorite politician is Vize Prezident, right? Hopefully he vill change zings for ze better between ze coloreds und ze vhites in ze zities."

"Yea, that's right, Annaliese. Teddy Roosevelt is President McKinley's Vice President. And I bet Teddy will win the Presidency in a few years with the next presidential election. I love the guy."

\*\*\*\*

"Hi, Lilly Ann. May I join you for lunch? I know the girls are kind of avoiding you because . . . well, because you're colored."

"It's okay, Miss Sophie. I'm used to it. And by all means, please, come join me."

"Thanks. I want you to know, Lilly Ann, that I'm not prejudiced at all. And I see you have a little pet here with you. Is that your cat?"

"Yes, this is my little Soteria; she's Abyssinian. She hasn't been feeling the best lately. I didn't want to leave her at home with my mother and two little ones, so I brought her to work. Miss Mittón said it would be okay, as long as the cat stays out of the way."

"Oh yes, the cat's fine. But if you don't mind, Lilly Ann, tell me about your kids."

"I have two: a boy, Thomas, and a girl, Sally Ann. The boy is the youngest, he's three. The girl is five. My mother, bless her heart, agreed to help me with the children after my husband died. He had the cholera. We came to New York from Louisiana. I have a friend here who said work was good in New York. So I figured me and my kids would do better up here rather than back home in the south, down around New Orleans. After Jim died—he was my husband—it really made a lot of sense to move up to New York. And I'm so happy to have found work at the millinery shop."

"Well, Lilly Ann, I'm sorry about your husband dying. I'm sure his support meant a lot. But that's great your mother is willing to help out with the children."

"Yes, for sure. And we have little Soteria here to protect us."

"Oh, is that so? Instead of being a watchdog, she's a watchcat?! Excuse me for chuckling, Lilly Ann, I just find that amusing. I don't mean to make fun."

"That's quite all right, Miss Sophie. Soteria is a very special type of cat to us. She was a gift, given to me by a houngan."

"A what?"

"A houngan—a voodoo priest—back home. He said she will always protect me, my family, and our home from pests. And she does just that. She catches mice, rats, and rodents, kills them and keeps them from coming into our house. She's pretty violent with them, but that's just fine with me. She can be an ornery little critter. Why, just last week, a wild dog came out of nowhere and snapped at our oldest kid. Bit her leg slightly, it wasn't too bad. But Soteria came down off the porch and chased the dog off into some nearby woods. I called her back. I didn't want her going into those woods. She might have gotten killed in there. Anyway, the cat came over to our daughter and snuggled up next to her. It was comforting."

"Oh, that's interesting, Lilly Ann. What a smart cat."

"Yes, we love her, our little Soteria. You know, her name—Soteria— is from Greek mythology, so I was told. She was the goddess of deliverance and protection. And Soteria certainly rules our household, like she's the queen."

"How nice. It's great to have such a wonderful pet. And it's been nice talking with you, Lilly Ann. We need to get back to work, but next time, I'll have to tell you a little bit about myself."

"I'd love that, Miss Sophie, and it's been nice talking with you to. But like you said, time to get back to work."

"For sure. By the way, Lilly Ann, what ever happened to that dog? Did he ever come back to bother the kids again?"

"You know, funny you should ask. Just a couple of days ago, they found the dog dead over in those woods. I was told his throat and neck was ripped to shreds, so much and so that the dog's head was nearly severed from its body. They figured it was either a wolf, a bear, or a wild cat like a cougar, so we've been warned to be very careful, especially in the evening or at night. But all's well that ends well."

"That's for sure, Lilly Ann, that's for sure. Well, back to work we go."

\* \* \* \*

"Good morning, Madame Mittón,"

"Good morning, girls. Please, take you seats. I have some very sad news for you today here on Monday, September 16, 1901. This is a date to remember, and a year to remember as well. Some of you may already know, President McKinley died this past Saturday from his gunshot wounds."

"Oh my God, Madame Mittón, I thought he was well on his way to recovering? At least that's what I read in the newspaper."

"Well, Mitzi, apparently a lot of newspapers were wrong. Or probably better to say they were misled by the president's doctors."

"I guess he must have suffered for a full week then, since he was shot on September 6 and that was a Friday. My goodness!"

"Yes, Mitzi, that's about right. Saturday was the fourteenth. It's very sad. He was just into his second term as president, and then that blasted anarchist had to shoot him. It makes me so mad. I hope that guy . . . what's his name?"

"Leon Czolgosz."

"Thank you, Sophie. You seem to have a knack for pronouncing some of these foreign names. Anyway, I hope that Leon What's-His-Name spends all eternity in hell."

"Well, Madame Mittón, there's one interesting aspect to all this."

"What is that, Sophie?"

"Mr. Rough Rider himself, our own Teddy Roosevelt, will become president."

"Yes, that's right, Sophie. Matter of fact, Mr. Roosevelt has already been sworn in, over in Buffalo where President McKinley was shot. You know he was attending some fair or exposition, I guess is what they call it. And you know—uh, yes Mitzi?"

"Madame Mittón, I read in one of the newspapers that the shooter, this Leon guy, was taken down by a Negro man, and he held the shooter down until the police took over. They say it likely kept the president from being shot more times."

"Zo, Madame Mittón, zee black man zaved zee vhite prezident'z life?"

"No, not exactly Annaliese. The president still died. But at least that Negro gentleman prevented more shots from being fired. I mean, someone else could have been shot too. I'd say that Negro fellow is a hero."

"I think we all agree to that, Madame Mittón. We all agree."

"Thank you for that, Sophie. And now, I do have more hat orders here, girls, that will add to your workload. So, time to get busy."

\* \* \* \*

"Hello, Annaliese. As always, thanks for comin' over to Miss Gordon's and spendin' time with me. By the way, I heard about the fire in the millinery shop."

"Yez, it iz . . . it iz vedy zad. Hold me, Adam, pleez."

"Honey, I'm ready to marry you if we can find someone who will do it. I want to take you away from this little hick town and bring you to my city. Rumor has it that the fire to your shop was started by the KKK, or some similar white hate group, 'cause of that colored girl, Lilly Ann, and the Jewish girl, can't remember her name."

"Rebecca."

"Okay, yes, Rebecca, and probably you."

"Me? Vhy me?"

"Can't you guess, Annaliese? Don't you know? They hate you because of me. But I'm ready, Annaliese, I'm ready to take you to my home, which will be our home, married or not."

"I'm ready too, Adam. Vhat, vee haf been zeeing each other for at leazt three yearz, no?"

"That's about right. This is 1904, and my hero has been president for three years, since McKinley died. Say, let's step outside, Annaliese. Too many ears around here in the lobby eatin' area."

"Ah, to be outzide iz nize. Weather iz great."

"Yea, Annaliese, let's walk along this path and just talk."

"Okay."

"You know, I believe President Roosevelt is goin' to go down in history as one of our greatest presidents. I admire that man so much that I would like to name my son—if I ever have one—after the president. My son's name would be Theodore Roosevelt Hart. Yep, that's what I would do."

"Vell, Adam, I'm ready to go to New York Zity with you. Und you just may haf zat opportunity to name your zon az you dezire. I'm pregnant vith your child."

*\*\*\**

"Annaliese, I just came by to wish you and Adam good luck in your move to New York City. I'm sure you two will make it, in spite of everything being thrown against you."

"Oh, zank you, Zophie. You been my bezt friend. Und ve'll continue to zee each other."

"Right, Annaliese, for sure. You know, the millinery shop has been rebuilt since the fire. But Madame Mittón seems to be losing interest in the shop, and in life itself. She does not look well."

"Perhapz you can run it for her, Zophie."

"Oh, I don't know, Annaliese, perhaps. By the way, there is something else. Last week, someone broke into Lilly Ann's house and tried to rape her."

"*Mein Gott*! Iz zhe all right."

"Yes, she's fine. Strangest thing, though, what Lilly Ann said. Their family's cat—I think her name is SodoTerry or something like that—she scared the intruder away! Lilly Ann says she thinks the cat scratched the guy's leg!"

"Goot. Did zee police catch him?"

"Well, sort of. They did catch up with him a few days later. He was found dead, laying in a grassy field. They know it was him because of the scratches on his leg from Lilly Ann's cat."

"That iz goot. How did he die?"

"His throat was ripped to pieces. Head nearly severed, so I was told. They figured a wolf or cougar probably got to him, although they're not sure. It was extremely vicious, and there hasn't been a sighting of any wolves, bears, or cougars around here in a couple years. Serves that would-be rapist right, I guess. There's been a number of attempted rapes of women lately. I believe I read or heard somewhere that two women were killed; can't recall their names though. Anyway, you and Adam enjoy your life together in the big city. And we'll see each other again, from time-to-time. We're not that far apart."

"Oh, Zophie, zank you, zank you for evryzing. Let me hug you. You are zee reezon I met Adam. Zank you, from zee bottom of me heart."

"And thank you, Annaliese, for being such a good friend over the years. I'll miss you, like I miss Emma. And Madame Mittón . . . well, I just miss the old crew. But speaking of crew, I'd better get back to the shop. It's late morning and I haven't even been in there yet. You take care, and maybe write when you can. Bye, Adam, bye, Annaliese."

\* \* \* \*

"Good morning, Madame Sophie."

"Good morning, ladies. Please, take your seats. I have some good news for you today. Now that we're in the Sears and Montgomery Ward catalogs, I have plenty of work orders for you from all over the country for our very fine hats and dresses!"

*Train Wreck at Montparnasse, France, 1895*

# THE BEST ROMANCE I NEVER HAD

Boy, if these folks on this train could read or hear my thoughts, they'd see and hear that I am having a long conversation with myself right about now. I'm just glad to be here. It seems like I've been traveling forever. Uh-oh, here comes the conductor. It looks like he's asking for tickets. Let's see, where did I put my blasted ticket?

"*Billets, s'il vous plaît! Puis-je avoir vos billets, s'il vous plaît!* For you Englize: Ticketz, pleez! May I have your ticketz, pleez!"

"Here you go, sir."

"*Merci, monsieur. Billets, s'il vous plaît! Puis-je avoit vos billets, s'il vous plait!*"

Well, that takes care of that. Perhaps I can catch me a little bit of shut-eye now. It has been a long trip for me already in this eventful year of 1905. Let me think now, let's see. I took a train from San Francisco to New York, then caught a freighter going across the Atlantic to France, and now here I am, on a train ride across the French countryside. But it's all good. I needed to get away for a very long vacation. Yes, the doctor said I needed it after all the stress of the presidential campaign that I worked so hard on. But it was worth it. Good old Rough Rider Teddy was elected president. And now that I think about it, he gave a great speech during his inaugural address this past March. I thought it was inspiring. I hope others did. Because we need to— whoa, we've made a station stop. And who is this beautiful brunette getting on the train? Aww, I better leave it alone till later. Let me shut my mind off and take a little nap.

"Ticketz pleez, m'dame."

"Oh yes, here you go. I really don't speak French, but I'm sure I'll pick a little bit up while visiting your beautiful country."

"Merci m—"

"You know, I'm from New York. I work at a hat shop; it's actually called a millinery shop. But we make elegantly fine ladies' hats and dresses, and I'm so excited on being here in France on vacation, and on a French train and all, to have a first-hand look at your gorgeous country! And . . . oh, I'm sorry, sir, Mr. Conductor, I'm keeping you from doing your job. I'm so sorry."

"*C'est tout à fait correct* . . . eh, it'z . . . ehh, quite all right, m'dame. *Je suis sûr que vous vous amuserez*. Eh, I'm zure m'dame will have fun. *Au revoir*."

"Yes, thank you, and ooovwah to you to."

*I've got to consult my little French-to-English translation handbook. I think it's somewhere here in my purse or bag. Oh shoot, I'll look for it later. I just need to lay back and rest for a bit, look around and admire the scenery, and . . . say, that's a nice-looking guy over there, asleep. Or is he pretending to be sleep? He had to see me when I came on the train. Oh well, let me grab this Harper's Weekly here that someone left and read up on what's going on in the old U.S. of A. Let's see, how old is this paper? Where's the date? I don't see the date. Oh, there it is — Saturday, June 24, 1905. And today is Wednesday, June 28th. So, this is the latest issue! Good. Looks like they have some interesting articles in here.*

"*Monsieur, rafraîchissements?*"

"Uh! What—what is it? You, you woke me up!"

"*Je m'excuse, monsieur*. Ehhh . . . r-r-refreshmentz?"

"No, thank you. I'm . . . I'm fine. Thank you."

*I must have really fallen asleep. I didn't realize that conductor was right next to me. And what a crazy dream! Let me see here,* that dream, that dream. Yea, I can piece it together. I was on a train, similar to what I'm riding in now. But it was . . . it was, uh, hazy? That's it, I'm sitting in my seat on a train, and the train car is filled with haze or a fog, or possibly smoke. I'm just not sure. But I do remember seeing several cats—yes, cats. I could see them through the haze or smoke. They were running down the aisle, heading toward the back of the train away from the front engine. I can't recall their faces, but man, they were running away from something, and running scared. Then the conductor wakes me up. I don't know what that dream means, if anything at all. It may be that it's because I'm on a train. And I do recall seeing a rather attractive lady on board, a colored woman with a pet cat. Yes, I do recall. The cat is white, and the woman is brown. She must have come up from east Africa, maybe Ethiopia? She has a pretty skin tone, kinda like a medium, smooth chocolate. But she is not as pretty as that brunette with the ivory-white skin. Let me see, where is she? Ahh, there she is, only three rows in front of me, across the aisle to my left. I'll have to keep a watchful eye on her. Oh man, what am I saying? I'm not her type. Let me get up from here, quit fantasizing, see if I can find that conductor and get me some—what'd he say? Oh yea—refreshments.

"Madame, vould yu like zome food? Madame—"

"Pierre, chut! Ne la réveille pas! Elle dort tellement bien. Nous reviendrons plus tard (Pierre, shhh! Don't wake her! She is sleeping so sound. We'll come back later)."

"Oui, d'accord (Yes, all right)."

"Tu vois, Pierre, elle bouge dans son sommeil (See, Pierre, she stirs in her sleep)."

"Oui, elle fait un rêve actif (Yes, she has an active dream)."

"Girls, it is so nice to have a picnic together after a long hard week of making hats and dresses and selling shoes and all that we do!"

"Yes, Mitzi, I agree! And I echo her sentiments, Madame Sophie. We really appreciate you allowing us to come together on such a lovely spring Saturday afternoon for a picnic."

"Well, thank you, Lilly Ann. I appreciate you, and you, Mitzi, and all of you fine ladies that have helped make our millinery shop the successful business that it is today. This year of 1905 is going to be a great year for us. Of course, we'll have to wait until Mitzi returns from her vacation trip to France this summer."

"Oh, Madame Sophie, please don't embarrass me like that."

"Mitzi, I'm just playfully teasing. We want you to have a wonderful time in France, enjoy that train ride you're planning, and meet some of those debonair Frenchmen. Maybe bring me back one! And Mitzi, I'll miss you very much. You're a fine worker, one of my best. Goodbye, Mitzi. Goodbye!"

"Madame? Madame, vould yu like zome food?"
"Uh? Oh, Jesus, you woke me up."
"*Je suis désolé*. Eh, I'm zorry. Vould yu like zome food?"
"Yes, yes I would. Boy, I was really having some dream."
"*Oui, m'dame*. Pleez, follow me."

My goodness, what a vividly real dream! It was as if I was back at that spring picnic from earlier this year. Gosh, we sure had a great time at that picnic! It was so nice of Madame Sophie to sponsor that event for us. I hope we can do it every year from now on. And the food was just delicious. Speaking of food, I guess I better eat what the, eh, train food preparers have served me. It looks good, roast beef with potatoes and carrots, bread and wine. One thing about that dream that bothers me though, now that I think about it. The parting goodbye said by Madame Sophie seemed so . . . well, so final. As if she was not expecting me back. But she never said it that way at the picnic. Matter of fact, I recall her saying that she and all the girls hope I enjoy my visit to France, and to hurry back to New York soon. They'll look forward to my return. I know, I remember quite well, that's what they said. Yet, in my dream here, there seemed to have been a feeling of finality from Madame Sophie. The way she said goodbye. Oh well, I'm not going to worry about it. Afterall, it was just a dream, my imagination running away with me. Probably meant nothing at all. Oh, there's that handsome gentleman again! I wonder why he won't speak to me. Maybe he's married. But he seems to be alone. I wonder if I should speak to him first. No, that would not be lady-like. Men are to pursue women, like dogs pursue cats. But cats can get away from dogs by climbing up a tree. Umm, that's a thought. Maybe I'm too high in a tree, figuratively speaking, and the handsome gentleman can't reach me. I'll have to give that more thought and see what sort of answers I can come up with. Well, let me get back into this Harper's Weekly. But shoot, I wonder what he is thinking about now! I'm sure he notices that I'm right here! I'll talk to him if he'll initiate the conversation. Maybe he's unsure of himself because of our differences. But we're in France, where people, even strangers, from everywhere talk all the time. So come on to me, you handsome devil you. I'm right here, waiting. He is keeping his head down, reading whatever he's into. Well, I'm not going to initiate the conversation. It's just not lady-like. He must speak to me first. So, back to my Harper's Weekly.*

"Ehh, your beverage, zir."
"Oh, thank you. Yes, very good. Thank you so much."
*"Vous êtes le bienvenu* (Your welcome)."

*Man, it is hard for me to get my mind off this lady across the aisle! God, she's pretty. Full breasts, beautiful skin, thick hair! She has it pinned up. I bet when she lets her hair down, it goes past her shoulders and touches her nipples . . . oh yeah, I can just see it through my mind's eye . . . nipples that glisten like the morning dew on gold buttercup flowers that sit atop exquisitely lovely breasts with the look of a snow-covered hill. God, would I love to play in that snow! Oh, let me stop, let me stop. I need to refocus my mind, get it off her. I see she's reading though. What is she reading? From here it looks like an issue of Harper's Weekly. Oh, it doesn't matter, I need to find something to read myself. I know, where is my copy of President Roosevelt's inaugural speech? I know I have a copy of it in my bag here somewhere. Ahh, yes, here it is.*

*This will take my mind off her. Okay, let's see. I'll just start at the beginning here. Let's see, let's see. Aww man, I'm just repeating myself and trippin' over my thoughts. Is she looking at me? I think she's looking at me. Should I say something to her? Should I say something to her? No, no, no, I can't! Let me stop this day dreaming. I'll just start reading his speech. This should get my mind off her:*

> "My fellow citizens, no people on earth have more cause to be thankful than ours, and this is said reverently, in no spirit of boastfulness in our own strength, but with gratitude to the Giver of Good who has blessed us with the conditions which have enabled us to achieve so large a measure of well-being and of happiness. To us as a people it has been granted to lay the foundations of our national life in a new continent. We are the heirs of the ages, and yet we have had to pay few of the penalties which in old countries are exacted by the dead hand of a bygone civilization. We have not been obliged to fight for our existence against any alien race; and yet our life has called for the vigor and effort without which the manlier and hardier virtues wither away. Under such conditions it would be our own fault if we failed; and the success which we have had in the past, the success which we confidently believe the future will bring, should cause in us no feeling of vainglory, but rather a deep and abiding realization of all which life has offered us: a full acknowledgement of the responsibility which is ours; and a fixed determination to show that under a free government a mighty people can thrive best, alike as regards the things of the body and things of the soul."

*Yeah, I just glanced over at her and she was looking at me! Caught her. But she doesn't look like she's interested in me. She just put her head back into that weekly newspaper.*

"Zir, are you finished with your beverage? Vould you like another, or may I have your glazz?"

"No, I'm done. Sure, here, you can have the glass. Thanks."

"*Merci, monsieur.*"

*I saw him look over at me. I think he wants me, but he won't come over and introduce himself to me! I wonder where he's going. Could we be going to the same destination? Jesus, he looks so muscular and strong. I bet he could pick me up off the bed, and . . . and . . . oh, let me stop, let me stop. C'mon, Mitzi, pull yourself together. There's nothing going on between you and this man. And nothing will be going on. Bring your focus back on the newspaper here. And it's a nice article about President Roosevelt's inaugural parade. Let's see, that happened back in March. Oh, wow, in the photo here as part of the parade are several Indians on horseback riding at the very front. That's interesting. Enemies yesterday, friends today. Let's see, does the article give their names and tribes? Oh yes, here it is. It lists them: Quanah Parker (Comanche), Buckskin Charlie (Ute), Hollow Horn Bear, American Horse (Sioux), Little Plume (Blackfeet), and Geronimo (Apache). My goodness, this is something, Geronimo in the president's parade! Wow, and the president was clapping his hands and waving his hat toward the Indians in appreciation. Now, I didn't know all that. Very interesting. I wonder if the girls back at the shop know this? Madame Sophie probably does. She stays up-to-date with this sort of thing. I think I'll take a short nap—but, all of a sudden, I have the strangest feeling! I feel like I'm being watched!*

"I'm sorry, ma'am. I think my cat was intrigued by the color of your clothes and that fine-looking bird and feathered hat you have there. I'll just pick her up and take her back to our seats. Now, now, that's a good kitty. We're visiting here from Boston. I've been planning for this trip to France for the past couple years. By the way, where did you buy that lovely hat?"

"Oh, ma'am, I *make* hats. This is my own custom design. I work in a millinery shop located in Schuylerville, New York. You know where that's at?"

"Yes, I think I do. Isn't it in the Saratoga region, where the race track is?"

"Yes, that's right. You got it. Let me get something to write with out of this bag. I have a little paper here too, somewhere in the bag. Give me a moment, please. I know those things are here in my bag somewhere. I just have to take a minute to find them."

"Oh, take your time, dear. That's quite all right. Take your time."

"Thank you. It shouldn't take me too much longer to find them. Ahh, there it is! I'll write down our address here for you . . . and the next time . . . you're up our way . . . please stop by, and . . . visit. Here you go."

"Why, thank you. I will. I will stop by. If your hat there is an example of the quality and style of hats that I might see at your shop, then I will definitely buy some hats from you. Thank you again. It's been nice talking with you and take care."

"Very well. I look forward to seeing you again, hopefully at our hat shop. Bye now."

> *Well, that's a nice lady. Maybe we'll have another new customer. That ought to really please Madame Sophie. I'm so glad that I decided to take this trip . . . me, little old Mitzi Schneider from upstate New York, traveling by train in France! Who would have believed it? And while here, I should pick up some great design ideas for lady's hats. Umm, come to think of it, my father was a Jewish tailor from Germany. With me being a designer and maker of women's hats, that kind of places me in a similar occupation as Pa-pa. If he was living and could see me now, he would be so proud of, and probably surprised at, my success in this millinery business—I mean, even if just as an employee! And speaking of surprise, I'd be surprised if this handsome gentleman across the way behind me would come over here and introduce himself to me. Maybe if I drop something on the floor. Would he make a move to pick it up and allow himself*

*to speak to me? Oh, shoot, I can answer that right now. His head is buried in whatever he's reading.*

"Say, conductor, when will we arrive at our next station stop?"

"In aboutz, ehh, twenty minutes, ve vill arrive at Orléans, zir. Zometime after zhat, zay just under two hours, ve vill arrive in Paree. Is zhere somesing I can do for you, zir?"

"No. I'll, uhh, I'll just continue my reading here. Thank you. Thank you very much."

"*Très bien. Au revoir* (Very well. Goodbye)."

*Okay. As I think about Teddy's opening remarks to this speech, he seems to be emphasizing how we are fortunate to inherit such a great legacy from our nation's forebears. And, as a free government of mighty people, it is our responsibility to continue that legacy. I sure hope he doesn't mean to continue the legacy of Negro subjugation . . . or does he? Let me read on.*

> "Much had been given us, and much will rightfully be expected from us. We have duties to others and duties to ourselves; and we can shirk neither. We have become a great nation, forced by the fact of its greatness into relations with the other nations of the earth, and we must behave as beseems a people with such responsibilities. Toward all other nations, large and small, our attitude must be one of cordial and sincere friendship. We must show—not only in our words, but in our deeds—that we are earnestly desirous of securing their good will by acting toward them in a spirit of just and generous recognition of all their rights."

*Okay, Mr. President, let me pause and think about this for a moment. This sounds noble, very worthwhile. But I wonder, does this apply to those nation's individuals that are different, such as in skin color? And especially when those, quote, unquote, "differences" live among us? I wonder.*

> "But justice and generosity in a nation, as in an individual, count most when shown not by the weak, but by the strong. While ever careful to refrain from wrongdoing others, we must be no less insistent that we are not wronged ourselves.
>
> We wish peace, but we wish the peace of justice, the peace of righteousness. We wish it because we think it is right, and not because we are afraid.
>
> No weak nation that acts manfully and justly should ever have cause to fear us, and no strong power should ever be able to single us out as a subject for insolent aggression."

*So far, so good there, Mr. President. But my eyes are getting tired. I think I'll stop reading for a while and focus on the scenery. And speaking of scenery, there's that pretty lady. And, oh my, she has that long dress pulled up slightly, and I can see a little bit of her leg and ankle.*

*Yeah, now we're getting into some good scenery. If she'll just hike it up a little more! Not too many others around in this train car just now. Just her and I actually, at least in this immediate area. My imagination is starting to get the best of me. Maybe, just maybe, I am her type. Oh, there's the conductor. He's in the way.*

"*Excusez-moi, madame. Voulez-vous une boisson?* Ehh, vould you like somesing to drink?"

"Yes, matter of fact I would. May I have a sarsaparilla?"

"*Oui*, I get for you."

"Great. Thank you."

*I know he's looking at me. I can feel it. You don't think I see you, fella, but I do, just out the corner of my right eye. He's checking out my leg. I think I'll play along with this game and hike my dress up a bit more. There! I want you to get an eyeful and then come talk to me.*

"*Pardon,* zir. Vould you like a beverage?"

"Yes, I would. I'll have whatever that lady over there is having. That looks good to me."

"Oh, over zhere?"

"Yes, over there."

"*Oui,* I get for you."

*Yeah, pretty lady, I see what you're doing. Reaching down to rub your ankle and lower leg. And, oh my God, is she beginning to put on a little private burlesque show for me! There is no one else around right now to see this but me. She won't look at me. It's as if she's all alone and no one is looking. But she must know I'm looking. And I'm doing a great job of it too. She's running her right hand up her dress, and left hand across her breast, and . . . ohhh . . . she's squeezing her right breast with that left hand! Through all that thick clothing, I wonder if she can feel herself. I can sure feel her. You've got my attention, honey, big time. And . . . uh-oh, here comes the conductor.*

"Madame, here'z your sarsaparilla drink. Ehh, are you okay?"

"Yes, yes, I'm fine, thank you. I . . . I just got a bit warm. This beverage should help to cool me down. Thank you. Just sit it down. I'm fine now. Let's see, where's that bathroom? Oh yes, I see it. Thank you. Let me just make my way to the bathroom. Excuse me."

*Awww! That Conductor interrupted a mighty good show. Of course, he didn't know what was going on. But I sure did. She's got me as hard as a rock. What am I going to do? I can't relieve myself right here. Will the noise of the train muffle my sound if I go off? No, no, no. I can't do this. Aww, here comes the conductor.*

"Zir, vould you like another beverage?"

"Yes, I'll have another, and this time with plenty of ice." *I think maybe I can put that ice to good use elsewhere on me.*

"Monsier, votre boisson. Ehh, your drink."

*Oh, my God, I hope no one can hear me in this bathroom. Maybe the train noise will muffle what I'm doing, and nobody will hear . . . what I'm doing. I hope I don't tear my panties and undergarments while doing this. I'm so wet, my fingers—wet. My cooty . . . uhh . . . cooty hole's wet. I want him to . . . oh Jesus, he's in my mind and in my fantasy, oh . . . oh . . . ohhh . . . aieeee . . . aieee! Tears! Why do I have tears? Why the tears? Is my innermost being that emotionally moved toward this man, such that my sexuality is crying out for him? Is my finger a substitute for his . . . his thing . . . ohhh . . . ohhh . . . aieee . . . aieee, oh God . . . Yes . . . Yes . . . Yeeessss! Uhh, uhhh, oh God, uhhh, uhhh . . . he's sooo good . . .uhh . . . aieee!*

"Mademoiselle, iz everyzing all right? Are you okay, Mademoiselle?"

"Yes, uhh, yes, uhhhh. Yes, yes, I'm fine. I'll be right out. I . . . was . . . just . . . having a bit of a dizzy spell. Maybe something I ate or drank. I'll be right out. I'm okay. Thank you."

"All right, Mademoiselle. Pleez, let me know if you need anyzing."

"Yes, yes, of course, I will. Thank you. I'll be out shortly."

*I wonder what she's doing in the bathroom. I sure wish I was in there with her.*

*That bathroom is small, the space tight, yes, very tight. I can imagine myself being in there with her. The little room becomes steamy. The mirror fogs up. I can imagine we're standing very close to each other, not kissing but our mouths are only an inch or two apart. I can feel her breath on my tongue, and she can feel mine on hers. I have an obelisk . . . long and thick. I turn to sit down on the toilet after dropping my trousers and underwear. She hikes up her dress, drops her undergarments and panties and shows me her glory. Oh God, it's beyond beauty . . . it's heavenly. Her supple skin is as white as the whitest clouds. Her lovely fine pubic hair covers a* pink gateway to immense, unimaginable pleasure. She sits on my lap, and we begin to . . .

"Zir, you've hardly touched your drink. Iz it okay? Ehhh, are you all right, zir?"

"Yes, yes, I'm fine. Thank you. I'll be all right. I was just having a bit of a dizzy spell there for a moment. Maybe something I ate or drank earlier. But I'll be fine. Thank you."

"All right, zir. Pleez, let me know if zhere iz anyzing I can do."

"Yes, for sure, I will. Thank you."

"*Tomas, c'est un peu étrange* (Tomas, this is a bit strange)."

"*Que veux-tu dire, Pierre?* (What do you mean, Pierre?)"

"*Cette dame ici et ce monsieur là-bas* (This lady over here, and that gentleman over there)."

"Quoi? Leur? (What? Them?)"

"*Quelque chose d'étrange à propos de ces deux-là* (Something strange about those two)."

"*Comme quoi?* (Like what?)"

"*Je ne peux pas dire avec certitude. Mais il y a un lien entre eux* (Can't say for sure. But there is a connection between them)."

"*Je pense que vous avez une mauvaise connexion* (I think you have a loose connection)."

"*Oui, retour au travail* (Yes, back to work)."

*Okay, back to my seat. Am I relieved? I . . . I think so. Let me get back into my Harper's Weekly. That guy, that man, it's all his fault. Why did he have to be on this particular train, the one I would be traveling on? All right, Mitzi, all right. Get a grip and get your mind off of him. Let's see what this article is all about. Let's see here, something about what Mark Twain says. Well, what does Mark Twain say? Okay, let's see. Oh, shoot! That guy has no idea how I'm feeling right now. God, I'm hot for him. I'm ready for him to undress me right now. I'd hold my breasts up for him to fondle and have his way with my nipples. I'd give him some, right here in this train's aisle, right now, right this minute if he wanted it. And I wouldn't care* who's looking. Goodness, my pantaloons are wet right where I want his thing to be. I can't believe this.

Mitzi, what is happening to you? I'm having this fantastic romance with him in my mind, and he won't even talk to me. Jesus, help me get my mind off this man! Perhaps if I have another cold drink with plenty of ice to cool me down—

"Mr. Conductor, sir! Hello, Mr. Conductor."
"*Quoi, mademoiselle?*"
"May I have another sarsaparilla, with plenty of ice?"
"*Oui, mademoiselle.* I get for you, right away."
"Thank you. I've been feeling so hot and dizzy. Perhaps that beverage will help."
"*Oui, bien sûr* (Yes, for sure)."

She seems to be uncomfortable, squirming and moving around in her seat. She can't hike her dress up anymore . . . there are too many train passengers back in their seats right next to us. Maybe she's sick and not feeling well. I see she's ordered another beverage. Perhaps I should too. No, I should just get back into reading more of Teddy's speech. It is interesting. He's saying some real nice things here, very humane. I wonder if she's interested in politics and this sort of stuff, like discussing the president's inaugural speech. No, I doubt it. She's kind of in her own world of fancy hats and stuff. I can imagine her snubbing a person like me. But what was that little show she put on just a little while ago? It seems like it was just for me, since no one else was around at the time. All right, I need to come back to reality. My imagination is running away with me. She was probably trying to entice me into a trap, like many of her kind are prone to doing. But then . . . oh, let me stop it. What else does the president say in his speech? Ah, here we go:

> "Our relations with the other powers of the world are important; but still more important are our relations among ourselves."

*Now I like that statement, Teddy. Very noble and very right. How do we get along with each other? A lot of them southerners need to take lessons on that. Anyway, good words, Teddy. Let's see how you continue:*

> "Such growth in wealth, in population, and in power as this nation has seen during the century and a quarter of its national life is inevitably accompanied by a like growth in the problems which are ever before every nation that rises to greatness.
>
> Power invariably means both responsibility and danger. Our forefathers faced certain perils which we have outgrown. We now face other perils, the very existence of which it was impossible that they should foresee. Modern life is both complex and intense, and the tremendous changes wrought by the extraordinary industrial development of the last half century are felt in every fiber of our social and political being. Never before have men tried so vast and formidable an experiment as that of administering the affairs of a continent under the forms of a Democratic republic. The conditions which have told for our marvelous material well-being, which have developed to a very high degree our energy, self-reliance, and individual initiative, have also brought the care and anxiety inseparable from the accumulation of great wealth in industrial centers. Upon the success . . ."

"Zir, ve vill be coming into the Gare Montparnasse station in Paree very zoon. Iz there anyzing elze I can get you?"

"No, I'm fine, thank you."

"*Oui, monsieur.*"

*Hmm, that station name, Gare Montparnasse, sure sounds familiar. I think there was a horrific train accident here, maybe some ten years ago? It made worldwide news. I have a pretty good memory for these kinds of events. I'm pretty sure that was it. But no matter, this is 1905 and safety measures have improved. Things are much better these days. And speaking of being better, I think I'll see if I can better my circumstances with the opposite sex by speaking to that pretty lady that I've been admiring—desiring—while on this train. I'll wait until she stands up, then I'll walk over and introduce myself to her, and we'll see what happens. Oh, there's that colored lady with the cat up there too, a few rows in front of my pretty white lady. Here I am, claiming something for me that ain't mine to claim.*

*Okay, looks like she's getting ready to stand up. I better get up now and start making my move.*

"*Mademoiselle,* do you need zome help? Pierre iz here to help you."

"No, Pierre, I'm fine. I'm just going to make my way to the restroom one more time before we arrive in Paris. And then, I'll—oh! Pierre, Mr. Conductor? I sense that the train is picking up speed. Shouldn't we be slowing down?"

"*Oui, mademoiselle.* I'll go zee what iz going on."

*All right, my pretty one, I'm coming toward you, and I hope we can connect! And—goodness, why is this train going so fast?*

"Kitty, come back here! Don't you run away from me! Goodness gracious me, come back here, kitty!"

*Man, I almost stepped on that lady's cat. Wonder why it's running from the front to the back? And now a couple of gentlemen right next to me are puffing away on their cigarettes, surrounding me in a haze of smoke. I've seen this picture before. Let me reach over to touch this pretty lady before she gets too far ahead of me. Goodness! This train is going way too fast, way too fast!*

"Mr. Conductor! Mr. Conductor! It's me, Mitzi. I'm scared. We are speeding way to fast! People are shouting back here. I'm beginning to hear screams, Mr. Conductor! Where are you? Jesus, we're going to crash! We're going to crash! Aieeee . . . Aieee . . . Aieee! Mary, Mother of God, save me . . . Oh, it's you, it's you! You . . . you finally came!"

\* \* \* \*

"*Dépêchez-vous, sortez ces personnes de cette épave et rendez-vous à l'hôpital* (Hurry, get these people out of that wreckage and to the hospital)."

"Listen, I'm a doctor. I speak English. I'm with the ambulance service to help sort through the bodies and any survivors. Do you recall if there were any Americans in this section of the train?"

"*Oui*, over here. These two."

"Quickly, quickly, let's see. Goodness! How is it that they ended up like that in this massive wreck?"

"*Je ne sais pas* (I don't know)."

"He's lying on his stomach and, let's see . . . yes, he's dead. This Negro gentleman is dead, with his left hand on the right breast of this white woman lying next to him. And she is on her back . . . and has her left arm coming up under his arm . . . with her hand on top of his hand . . . as if she is holding his hand to her breast. Were they married, this interracial couple?"

"*Non monsieur, ils n'étaient pas mariés. Mais d'une certaine manière, je pense qu'ils étaient connectés d'une manière étrange* (No sir, they were not married. But somehow, I think they were connected in some strange way)."

"Wait a minute, wait a minute. She's breathing, she's still breathing. She's alive! Hurry! Get that stretcher over here. Let's get her out of this mess right away. My God, she's alive. It's a miracle, but she is alive!"

\*\*\*\*

"Hi, Mitzi. How are you feeling after such a long trip, and given what happened and all?"

"Oh, Lilly Ann, I'm doing all right. It's great to be back home in New York, even though I'm not quite all the way home to Schuylerville just yet. But being just outside of New York City and in this particular wing of the hospital is great. They're treating me well. And I'll soon be back at work. But Lilly Ann, I came across this guy, he was a Negro, as handsome as any man could be. And sexy beyond belief. We didn't meet, we didn't talk. But my imaginary romance with him was absolutely wonderful. It was the best romance I never physically experienced with a man. I was told he was killed in the train accident we were in. Very sad.

I really would have liked to have known him. It seemed like he was a very bashful guy. Maybe he didn't want to approach me because of the racial thing, you know? He being colored and me being white. But that was France, not America. Colored people are treated with so much more respect over there. In France, they have dignity. But here in America . . . oh well, let me leave that alone. Anyway, I was quite sad to hear that he didn't make it out okay."

"Mitzi, I'm afraid I have some more very sad news for you. I waited a few days before coming down here to visit you. I wanted to be sure you were strong enough to handle this."

"Goodness, Lilly Ann, what is it? Please, tell me. I'm okay."

"Well, Mitzi, you weren't the only one from the millinery shop that was involved in a train accident. Madame Sophie was on a train, heading down to Baltimore to visit some relatives, when it jumped the track about thirty-five miles just outside of Baltimore. It hit another train and both trains went off the rails. Thirteen people were killed. Madame Sophie was one of them. I'm so sorry Mitzi, I'm so sorry. The millinery shop will never be the same."

*Acer cappadocicum spring*

# THE FACE IN THE LEAVES

" Lilly Ann, can you spare a minute during break time?"

"Sure, Rebecca. It's almost break time now. I don't think Madame Mitzi would mine if we took our break now. You ready?"

"Yes, let's go outside."

"What's on your mind, Rebecca?"

"Lilly Ann, I've noticed that ever since we started working here together at the millinery shop, you've carried yourself in such a dignified manner, in spite of how others treat you because you're colored. And I admire that, I really do."

"Why, thank you, Rebecca. I do my best to treat others the way I'd like to be treated—the Golden Rule, you know."

"Yes, I know. I also noticed another good quality in you."

"Oh? What's that?"

"You are a good listener, and when you do speak, what you say always sounds so wise and makes a lot of sense. I admire you greatly, I do."

"Why, thank you, Rebecca. I didn't know I had such an ardent admirer in you."

"Yes, yes. And it's because of my great admiration for you, Lilly Ann, that I feel I can talk to you about a confidential matter with regard to my family."

"Goodness, Rebecca, you have really caught me off guard! Although I'm quite flattered. I never knew you felt this way about me. I consider it an honor. But I don't know if I can be of much help."

"I think you're just the person that can help me, Lilly Ann. Over these past few years, with the passing of Madame Mittón and Madame Sophie, the people I've always looked up to seem to always leave us too soon."

"Well, Rebecca, I plan on being around a long time. But speaking of time, I don't think we will have enough of it to discuss what's bothering you right now. We'll have to get back to our work tables."

"Yes, ma'am, I agree. We need to get back to work. But sometime soon, can we . . . ?"

"You don't even have to finish that sentence, Rebecca. Tell you what: why don't you come over to my house after work this evening? You can have dinner with us . . . you know, me, the kids, and Soteria, our wonderfully protective cat. And then you and I can talk privately for as long as we want. My mother is away right now, so we don't have to worry about an extra set of ears listening in. How's that sound?"

"That sounds wonderful, Lilly Ann! There's nothing I need to do at home after work, so I can come straight to your house."

"Good! Then it's settled, you come home with me after work. The kids should be home from school."

"Yes, thank you, Lilly Ann, thank you so much. I look forward to talking with you."

"And I look forward to hearing what you have to say. See you after work, Rebecca."

\* \* \* \*

"Well, here we are, Rebecca. Make yourself comfortable. Sit anywhere you like. Let me get some dinner together for the kids. There are chairs and a small table in their bedroom for them to eat from. We can stay here in the dining area and eat and have our private conversation."

"That sounds fine, Lilly Ann. You go right ahead and do what you have to do. I'm in no hurry to eat. By the way, where's your cat, umm, what's its name?"

"Soteria; her name is Soteria. She's in the bedroom with the children. She's like our family's watchdog, you might say, only much better than a dog. I'll be right back."

"Take your time, Lilly Ann. I'm in no hurry, and—oh, that was quick! I looked away for just a minute as you left, and the next minute, you're right back!"

"Well, it didn't take long to get the kids and Soteria settled. Let's you and I eat and talk."

"Okay, Lilly Ann, but I do want to ask you about your pet cat, Soteria."

"Sure, go ahead, ask away while I eat on this stew I made. I think you'll like it."

"I'm sure I will. But a question or two for you. I've never heard of a cat being some kind of guard dog, for heaven's sake. I mean, what can a cat do, besides scratch and bite a little bit? A wolfhound would practically eat a cat alive, wouldn't it?"

"Let me just say this, Rebecca. Soteria is a very special kind of cat . . . totally different from other cats. A wolfhound, or any other type of animal for that matter, would be no match for her. Soteria has a keen sense of danger-detection when it comes to our family, and she will do whatever is necessary to remove that threat. That's why she is our queen and all-encompassing protector of this household!"

"Okay, Lilly Ann. I still don't quite see how such a small cat could do such great things! Where did you get her from, anyway? I might like to have a cat like her."

"She was a gift to me from — how shall I say? — a holy man, down in my home in Louisiana. But enough about Soteria! Let's talk about what it is that's bothering you. Maybe I can help you, and maybe I can't. But I can at least hear everything you've got to say. So, shoot!"

"All right. Thank you, Lilly Ann, I appreciate your time. By the way, you have a lovely place here. And your stew is delicious!"

"Why, thank you, Rebecca. And I thought you might like that stew."

"Well, as you can probably guess from my name, my family and I, we're Jewish."

"Yes, Rebecca, I figured as much. But there's certainly nothing wrong with being Jewish, is there? I know there are those who are anti-Semitic, anti-Negro, anti-Irish, and anti-whatever. After all, this is America, land of the free . . . but only for those who are privileged to be white

Anglo-Saxons. The rest of us be damned. That's just the way it is right now, Rebecca. That's just the way it is."

"Yes, I . . . I know that, Lilly Ann. But what I would like to know is how you and your people, being colored, handle the discrimination and downright cruelty you are made to endure. I mean, I have relatives . . . my twin sister, Shiphrah, for example, she has a twelve-year-old girl, my niece, Rachel, who was seven years old at the time when Mother Jones had her children's march from Philadelphia to New York, marching to President Roosevelt's house to protest the abusive practice of child labor. That was in 1903, Lilly Ann—1903! If my memory serves me correctly, President Roosevelt didn't even *meet* with Mother Jones! And what was it, just a couple years ago I think, in 1906, the president got a Nobel Peace Prize I think it was? But he could not make peace with Mother Jones and those children?! Now, here we are in January 1908, and things aren't too much different. We cannot worship on Shabbat, which for us begins every Friday evening, we cannot observe it like we want because some of my family must work like slaves during that time. And it is really beginning to affect my niece, Rachel."

"My goodness, Rebecca. In what way is she being affected?"

"Through dreams, Lilly Ann. She has these terrible dreams. I guess you might say they're nightmares in some ways. But she calls them just 'bad dreams.'"

"What kind of bad dreams is she having?"

"Something about seeing a face, or maybe faces, in the leaves of a tree. I need to first give you a little background on Jewish folklore, about creatures we call leviathans. They can be found in —"

"Mommeee, we're done eating."

"All right, kids. I'll be right there. Let me tend to these children, Rebecca. Then I'll be right back."

"Yes, I understand, go right ahead. I'll chew down a few more mouthfuls here while you tend to your children. By the way, let me just say again, Lilly Ann, this is *excellent* stew. The meat is so tender, tastes like lamb."

"Yes, it is lamb. Soteria brought it to us."

"Huh? What?!"

"Um . . . I . . . just kidding, Rebecca. Of course, I was just kidding about that. Yes, well then . . . I'll be right back."

\* \* \* \*

"Sorry about that, Rebecca, I'm back now. Please, continue what you were about to say."

"Okay. Well, Lilly Ann, our Jewish holy scriptures, what we call the *Tanakh* —and what you call the Old Testament — has many verses that describe, or in some way mention, behemoths or monsters. In most cases, they are referred to as leviathans."

"Yes, I've heard that term — leviathan — mentioned from the Bible, like you say. I consider it part of the symbolism for which the Bible is noted for."

"For sure, the Bible is full of symbolism. But there is a member of our family, Benjamin, or Uncle Ben, he loves to fashion tall tales and scary stories for the children in our large family by using some of that symbolism from the Bible. I mean, in the minds of these kids, he creates images of these dinosaur-type monsters! He has them hiding in the trees or under the trees. And he backs these images of huge, tree-dwelling monsters by referencing scriptures somewhere in Job. Some of these kids become so scared, that —"

"Wait a minute, Rebecca. Let me get this straight. Now, admittedly, I am not a student of the Bible. However, I always thought that the terms 'leviathan' or 'behemoth' were references for large lizards and alligators, like what you see in the bayous and swamps of the South. But here, you're saying these terms in the Bible really pertain to pre-historic dinosaurs?"

"Well, not exactly . . . although that *could* be, Lilly Ann. What I am saying is that this uncle tells these scary stories to the children using monster-like imagery he pulls from the Bible. And it's believable to the kids. To them, those monsters are real because it's from the Bible, and the Bible doesn't lie, it's truth. They don't see, or they can't grasp yet, the symbolic nature of those creatures, even though several adults have tried to explain it to them and have really gotten on my uncle's case about these stories. But he keeps telling them, and the children seem to love to be scared . . . except for one."

"You know, Rebecca, I think I'd be scared too if I was a child, being told these strange stories about monsters in trees and such. Bible or no Bible, to a little kid, that can be pretty scary."

"I don't disagree with you, Lilly Ann. And Rachel seems to be the one that is most scared of these stories. She's the exception I was referring to. She doesn't want to hear those stories anymore because she is having nightmares about them, or at least that's what my sister tells me."

"Oh, my goodness! What sort of nightmares?"

"Well, from what my sister says, things start out as a rather simple dream..."

\* \* \* \*

"Aieeeeee! Mommy! Mommy! Aieeeeee! Aieeeeee!"

"Rachel, Rachel, stop that screaming, honey! Mommy's right here, baby. It's all right. It's all right. Mommy has her arms around you. My goodness, you are really trembling. What's wrong, baby? Did you have another one of those nightmares?"

"Yes, Mommy. But it wasn't just a nightmare; it was real! I saw it, right outside my bedroom window—*there*, right *there*! It was real, Mother, it was real!"

"Yes, honey, okay. I'm going to *insist* that Ben stop telling you children those awful stories!"

"But Mommy, I haven't listened to Uncle Ben's stories in a long while. I guess they're still in my head. But my dreams also include that awful, smelly, dirty factory where I worked, and how badly we were treated as Jewish children! This is just before we marched with Mother Jones."

"Okay, okay. It's all right. You can stop crying, Rachel, and let's talk this out. Maybe that's the best way to shake off these nightmares, to talk about them. So, go ahead. Tell Mommy your entire dream, as best as you can remember. Mommy's listening."

"Well, it starts out with me working in the factory like I used to do. Although in the dream, it is much darker than the way it was at the factory. I'm working away at my little bench, sorting through these machine parts, just like I was told to do. When all of a sudden, I hear screams. It's Timmy, he got his fingers caught in one of the machines and he loses two fingers, I think from his left hand! He's looking straight at me, screaming in pain! There's blood everywhere. I look at the machine where he was working, and it looks like one of those monsters Uncle Ben always tells stories about."

"I *knew* I needed to tell Ben a long time ago to quit telling those scary stories! Go on, Rachel."

"Well, Mommy, after I look at the machine that begins to look like one of those monsters, the picture changes and I'm back in my bed, looking out the window at the tree out back. Everything seems to be fine, until it starts to get dark, very dark outside. But I can still clearly see the tree and the leaves. The wind starts blowing, causing the tree limbs and leaves to rustle and move about. Next thing I know, the leaves really begin to move about, in circles. And then, it's like something moves them along the ground and they—the leaves—begin to come up the backside of the house. And when they reach my bedroom window, there's this face in the leaves, this awful, weird, animal-like face. Mommy, I'm scared! *I'm scared!*"

\* \* \* \*

"Wow, Rebecca, that is some weird dream your niece had. I mean, this is how your sister described it to you?"

"Yes, Lilly Ann, that is exactly how my sister described Rachel's dream. And it's happened more than once. Not every night, but more than they would like. Well, like I said earlier, Lilly Ann, I trust your advice. What do you suggest we do, or what should my sister, Shiphrah, do?"

"Rebecca, I'll have to sleep on this one and get back to you. It's getting late. I'll get you a hansom cab to take you home. I don't want to see you walking home at this time of night. But before you go, would you mind taking a few minutes to tell me about your sister's name, Shiphrah? That is a very interesting name. I've never heard it before. With your family being Jewish, I suspect it has some sort of connection or meaning to your faith? Do you mind?"

"No, Lilly Ann, not at all. I don't mind a bit. It is, indeed, a biblical name found in the first chapter of Exodus. I think that's the only place it is found in the entire Bible . . . both the Old and New Testaments, as Christians call them."

"Wait a minute, Rebecca, you don't call them Old Testament and New Testament?"

"No. As I mentioned earlier, Jews refer to the Old Testament as the *Tanakh*. Now, I'm no expert when it comes to Jewish studies of scripture, but I can share some basic things. We sub-divide the *Tanakh* into three sections: the *Torah*, which spans from Genesis to Deuteronomy and encompasses our laws, also known as the Five Books of Moses; the *Nevi'im*, which includes the books of Judges and Prophets; and the *Ketuvim*, which are all the writings in Psalms, Proverbs, and several other books. The word *Tanakh* is an acronym of these three sections: T for *Torah*, N for *Nevi'im*, and K for *Ketuvim*. As Jews, we don't recognize or accept the New Testament as divinely inspired scripture. "

"Wow! Okay, one learns something new every day! But, please, Rebecca, continue. This is all very interesting."

"Sure. Are you familiar with the story of Moses and how he was saved from being killed as a newborn?"

"Well, sort of. Wasn't he pulled out of a river — I guess, maybe, the Nile? — by somebody in Egypt?"

"Yes. As the story goes, he was pulled out of the Nile River by the daughter of Egypt's king, whom they called Pharaoh. This Pharaoh had issued a decree that all male Hebrew children were to be killed immediately after they were born. The females could be kept alive. But these were—"

"Wat a minute, Rebecca. Why were only the males to be killed?"

"Oh, Lilly Ann, that's a long story, I think! I can't relate all of the details behind it accurately. Like I said, I am not all that scholarly about Jewish scriptures. But, if my childhood memory is correct, it seems that Pharaoh believed that the Hebrews, as they were called back then, were becoming so numerous that they would one day rise up and overthrow him. So he wanted all the male babies killed. You're nodding your head, so I guess you are following my story okay?"

"Yes, I am! I follow you. Please, continue."

"Well, the midwives who were charged with the responsibility of delivering the babies did not obey Pharaoh's decree, and they spared the male Hebrew babies from being killed. Shiphrah was one of those merciful midwives. Her name means "beauty and splendor." My sister nearly died after we both were born. Some kind of heart ailment, I think. Anyway, the midwife who waited on my mother was able to keep my sister alive until more expert medical help could arrive. Mother was so grateful that she felt inspired to name my sister Shiphrah, after the midwife of the Bible in Exodus, and in honor of the midwife who kept my sister alive just like Shiphrah did with Moses."

"What a beautiful story, Rebecca. Thank you for sharing. Maybe someday I might have the opportunity to meet your sister and niece. But for now, let's get you that horse and buggy to take you home."

"Thank you, Lilly Ann. I'm sure you'll meet my family one of these days. And it's very nice of you to get me a hansom cab. I really don't mind walking though."

"No, no, no, I insist! You never know if some rapist is out there ... until it's too late. I'll get you a ride. Meantime, I'll be talking with you about some ideas you can share with your sister and her daughter. One thought is to confront the image, even in the dream. Rather than run from it, go toward it and see what it's all about. It might not be as bad as it might look, or as one might think. Just one thought. We'll talk later."

"I don't know if a child—or even an adult, for that matter—could manage to find the strength to walk *towards* something they're afraid of. But all right, Lilly Ann. Bye for now!"

* * * *

"Here you are, ma'am. The other lady already paid your fare, she did. You best get along now and get indoors. It's dangerous for young women like you to be out on the streets on a night like this. So please, get indoors right away."

"Yes, sir, I will; I'm heading to my door now. Thank you very much, thank you. Goodnight."

"Goodnight, ma'am."

* * * *

"Good morning, Madame Mitzi."

"Good morning, ladies. Please, take your seats. I have some good news for you. I have here, in this large box, literally dozens upon dozens of orders for hats and dresses — custom-made! — for several groups of sea-faring women going to the 1908 Olympic Games at the end of April in London. Let's see, this is late January, so we've got a couple months to get these orders filled and have the merchandise ready for customer pick-up by, say, the first week of April."

"Thank goodness we seem to be having a fairly mild winter so far, Madame Mitzi."

"Yes, Lilly Ann, that is definitely in our favor. Everyone should be able to get to work okay. Now, here is how I want to divide up the workload. Lilly Ann, I want you to . . . to . . . Oh, my God, my God! Annaliese? *Annaliese!* It's Annaliese that has just come through the door, like a specter from the past! Annaliese! Come here and let me give you a big hug! I haven't seen you in ages, Annaliese."

"Yez, Mitzee, it'z been a long time. Hello, eveyone. It iz zo good to zee all of you, zome once again, and zome for zee firzt time. Mitzi, Rebecca, Lilly Ann, und zo many new faczes. My, how zee millinery zhop haz grown. Und, Mitzi, you are . . ."

"Yes, Annaliese, I'm the new owner . . . lock, stock and barrel. I'll have to bring you up to date on how we've been doing! Let me introduce you to the ladies we've hired since you've been gone. But first, tell me, I take it this little fella is your boy?"

"Yez, thiz iz our little four-year-old ZeodoreZeodore . . . Zeodore Roozevelt Hart. You know, the prezident is Adam'z hero, zo he vanted to name our firzt child, if he waz to be a boy, after Prezident Roozevelt."

"All right, very nice! Here, let me introduce you around. How long are you able to stay?"

\* \* \* \*

"Zank you, Mitzi, for having uz over for dinner. You have a nize plaze here."

"Thank you, Annaliese, for having dinner with me! And little Theodore here is a nice, quiet little fella. May I call him Theo for short?"

"Zhure, that'z fine. Zounds cute."

"He doesn't seem to talk much. He's not like one of these chatty children who don't know when to shut up and be quiet . . . to be seen and not heard."

"Yez, Mitzi, he doezn't talk too much, ezpecially around otherz. At home though, around me und Adam, he can be very talkative."

"Yes, I'm sure. Speaking of Adam, how is he?"

"He iz fine . . . traveling down in Zouth America, avay from zis northern cold. He findz and evaluatz raze horzes. You know, that iz hiz job, vorking vith raze horzes."

"Yes, I remember. Have you settled into New York okay? I recall they've had some tough racial incidents in recent years, since your boy's namesake has been president. And, you know, with you and Adam being an interracial couple and all . . . and now with a racially mixed kid, I imagine things are pretty difficult for you, Adam, and little Theo. Right? I mean, it seems like the racial divide in our country is worsening, getting wider and wider, and not just in the South, but all over, even out west with other races, like the influx of Chinese. They're treated horribly, from what I've heard and read."

"Yez, Mitzi, that'z right. You know, I . . . I love Adam, very much. But it haz been a tough go of it for me und him. Ve are looked upon vith zuch zcorn. Even from new immigrant arrivals . . . Irish, Italians, Norzern Europe, it iz amazin' how quickly the racism so common in America becomz zo quickly common among zeese new arrivalz."

"How right you are, Annaliese. You know, this is an election year, and President Roosevelt is through. I hear President Roosevelt is supporting Howard Taft as the Republican nominee to be his successor."

"I zuppoze. I don't keep up vith politicz, Mitzi."

"Well, Annaliese, I sure do because it directly affects our business of creating unique hats for women. I mean, with all the political gala events such as inauguration balls, masquerade balls, parties, conventions, and so on, the ladies are going to want to sport their own unique style of hats. And we are very good at accommodating a lady's unique and unusual taste."

"Oh, yez, yez, yez. I haven't forgotten from vhen I vorked zhere. Zhe millinery zhop iz zecond to none!"

"That's right! And we've maintained that standard over the years. But back to the racial divide. I recall what happened to President Roosevelt several years ago when he tried to bridge that divide. You remember?"

"No, nutzing comz to mind. Vhen I zink back to zhoze earlier yearz, I'm reminded of Zophie and it makez me too zad, Mitzi. You best tell me vhat you remember."

"I understand, Annaliese. We all loved her and miss her greatly. But what I was recalling when—I think it was in 1901 or 1902—President Theodore Roosevelt invited the Negro leader Booker T. Washington to the White House for dinner."

"Oh, yez, yez, Mitzi. I remember zat. All hell broke looze."

"That's right, it sure did. All hell broke loose. I mean, the white supremacists crazies came out of the woodwork from everywhere, all over the country, but especially in the South. Down there, it appeared to me that the lynching and beating of Negroes escalated to new heights—that are *still* escalating to this very day! The racial division bothered President Roosevelt, so I don't think he tried inviting Mr. Washington back. I did hear that he and his family invited Negro leaders to their private resident in New York. But I don't think he tried doing that at the White House ever again."

"Yez, I'm zhure you're right, Mitzi. You know, Adam lovez Prezident Roozevelt; he practically vorships him. But right now, more of our conzern iz vith neighborhood gangz, especially Italian, und how it iz affecting our little boy, Zheodore."

"Oh, my goodness, Annaliese. Is it that bad?"

"Yez, Mitzi, it iz zat bad, und getting vorze. It iz becoming a challenge for Zheodore to play outzide without being harazzed by a gang of older Italian boyz. Und Zeo, he iz having nightmarz, zeeing zheze boyz facez in the treez as grotezque figurz."

"Goodness, Annaliese, what a strange coincidence."

"Vhat do you mean, Mitzi?"

"One of the girls at the shop, Rebecca, she has a twelve-year old niece who is bothered with similar nightmares. At least that is what Rebecca told Lilly Ann, and Lilly Ann shared it with me. The little girl also sees faces ... wild, cat-looking, monster-type faces in the leaves of the trees. The little girl is really suffering with those nightmares."

"Zhe being tvelve yearz old makez her much older zan my Zheo. I mean, zhe iz almozt a teenager, and vill be one in anozher year or two."

"Yea, Annaliese, that is true. So, what are you driving at?"

"Perhapz Rebecca'z zizter zhould take her daughter to zee a doctor—you know, zhat dealz vith zhe mind, maybe? I vould zink zhe zhould be outgrowing zhis zort of zing."

"Well, maybe someone like a psychiatrist might help rid her of those nightmares. I'll mention it to Rebecca, or to Lilly Ann to suggest to Rebecca. Meantime, it is getting late."

"Yez, Mitzi, you're right, it iz getting late and vee'd better getz back to our boarding room. I'll talk to you again vhen vee meet, okay?"

"For sure, Annaliese, let's plan to get together! I'd love to hear more. Meantime, take care and say hello to Adam for me."

"I vill. Bye now."

"Goodbye, Annaliese. It was sure nice visiting with you. Bye!"

\* \* \* \*

"Adam, it iz good to have you home for Chriztmaz."

"Well, it is good to be home, Annaliese, to see you and our little Theodore. I know I've been gone a long time down in South America and all. But I have to begin gettin' geared up for the 1909 horse racing season, which is just around the corner."

"Yez, my dear, I underztand. Und I'm zhure our little Zheo underztandz vhen I explain to him vhere you are. You know, I've ztarted calling him Zheo for zhort. Mitzi started that, und I like it. Und so does he."

"Yea, it does seem to fit him. You like that, son, being called Theo for short?"

"Yes, daddy, I likes it."

"He talks so well, Annaliese. He must get that from you, in spite of your heavy German accent."

"Oh, I don't know about zat, Adam. He probably getz a little bit from both of uz. But right now, my little *junge*, it iz time for you to go to bed. C'mon, letz go."

"Awww, mommy, I want to stay—"

"*Nien!* Bedtime for you, little one. Tell you vhat: I vill zing a little bit of a German Chriztmaz carol for you, in itz original verzhion. Zo, let'z go, c'mon, *gehen, gehen!*"

"Okay, mommy, I'm ready to hear the, um, song. I'm a little scared."

"Vhy, Zheo, vhy are you zcared?"

"I saw faces in the Christmas tree mommy. I saw them looking at me."

"Oh, honey, zat vas probably juzt your reflection off zee ornamentz. Ziz zong vill help you go to zleep und help you feel better. Now, zis iz a very old German Chriztmaz carol, not American, written by Herr Jozeph Mehr zome ninety yearz ago. You ready?"

"Yes, mommy, I'm ready."

"Okay. I vill firzt zing it in German for you, zhen in Englizh. Okay?"

"Okay, mommy."

> ♪ *Stille Nacht! Heilige Nacht!*
> *Alles schläft, einsam wacht.*
> *Nur das traute heilige paar. Holder knab im lockigten haar,*
> *Schlafe in himmlischer ruh! Schlafe in himmlischer Ruh!*
>
> ♪ Zilent night! Holy night! All are zleeping, alone
> and awake.
> Only the intimate holy pair. Lovely boy with curly hair,
> Zleep in heavenly peace! Zleep in heavenly peace!

"Is he sleep?"

"Yez, dear, Zheo iz zleep."

"Good! Now come to bed with me, Annaliese. I need you to stand over me, buck naked, and begin to sing *me* to sleep, along with a little somethin' else . . . and yes, in the nude!"

"Ooooh, Adam, you bad dog. I love it!"

\* \* \* \*

"Rebecca, why don't we have Madame Mitzi join us for lunch. She's been trying to reach out to each employee, spending one-on-one time with us, to get to know us better and become more acquainted with our individual skills, personalities, likes and dislikes, even our families. I think she believes it helps to create a more positive and productive work environment. And I agree with her. What do you say?"

"Yes, Lilly Ann, that's fine with me. I would like to hear what Madame Mitzi has to say, her opinion and thoughts, on some of my family's issues that I described to you. Let's do it."

"Great! However, there is something I think you ought to consider, Rebecca."

"Oh? What is that?"

"Remember when Madame Mitzi was involved in that horrible, horrible train crash in Paris, France a few years ago?"

"Yes, absolutely, I do. I remember it quite well. It's a miracle that she survived. She said a fellow passenger, a man she never really had the chance to know, was killed. I think she would have liked to have gotten romantically involved with him, if my memory serves me correctly."

"Yes, Rebecca, you're right. She did say something along those lines. Well, I think we ought to go easy on explaining the nightmare dreams of your niece to Madame Mitzi, you know? The descriptions of darkness and the horror-type imagery might trigger vivid memories of her train accident."

"Oh, yea, I . . . I hadn't thought of that, Lilly Ann."

"Right. I know Madame Mitzi is older than us, and she's quite mature. But remember, it took her a while to recover emotionally and psychologically from that whole horrific experience. And I don't want her to have a relapse."

"I agree, you're right, Lilly Ann. I'll watch what I say."

"Good, me too. We'll invite her to have lunch with us tomorrow."

\* \* \* \*

"Thank you, Lilly Ann and Rebecca, for inviting me to have lunch with you today. You could not have picked a better spring day here in April of 1909. It is pleasantly warm, with a gentle breeze."

"Thank you for coming, Madame Mitzi. We are delighted that you could join us."

"No, Lilly Ann, it is I who am grateful that you would ask me to join you for lunch. You both have been good, steady workers at the millinery shop for a number of years. I think it's been about nine years now, and you both are quite good in your hat creations."

"Well, we try, Madame Mitzi. And, yes, it will be nine years come this August. But we still try hard to do a good job."

"Of course, Rebecca, I know you do. And the job you both have done in your time at the shop is commendable. But the times have caught up with us, and we are going to have to make some changes. However, I will tell you both about that when we have an employee meeting. I need to share these changes with everyone. But tell me now, while I eat on this sandwich, how have you ladies been doing, and how are your families?"

"Well, Madame Mitzi, I'm doing okay. My children are fine and healthy. And our cat, Soteria, is great company for our family. I still get the usual scowl looks from people, especially white women, because I am colored. The white guys tend to stare at me as well. But I think their stares are more motivated by, how shall I say, uhmmm . . . I think their stares come from a deep-seated sexual passion, rather than racially-based malcontent like the women. You know, I just take it all in stride. Even though I'm a colored woman, I have the same physical equipment as a white woman."

"And better put together than most women, I might add, Lilly Ann—white or brown! You have God-given beauty."

"Oh, my goodness, thank you, Madame Mitzi."

"How about you, Rebecca, our pretty little red head? Life treating you well?"

"Yes, Madame Mitzi, I'm doing okay. But one of my nieces, Rachel, has been troubled with reoccurring nightmares. And I'd like to get your opinion on how we possibly can help her get over them."

"Of course, Rebecca, of course. I recall Lilly Ann telling me — oh, maybe late last year? — she told me a little bit about what your niece was going through. But please, fill me in. What brought these nightmares on?"

"My niece, Rachel, was heavily involved in child labor, Madame Mitzi. She even marched with Mother Jones. I think the nightmares started when one of the young boys, at the factory my niece worked at, had a terrible accident on one of the machines. He lost a couple fingers, and Rachel saw him . . . and heard him . . . scream in horrific pain."

"I would think that would be quite traumatic for any child, Rebecca. I certainly can understand how witnessing such a horrific event could trigger nightmares. But please, continue, Rebecca."

"Yes, Madame Mitzi, it *was* quite traumatic for little Rachel. To her, that factory then became very dark and eerie. The machines took on the imaginative form of trees in Rachel's mind. Like trees in a forest with the knobs, dials, and handles on their front side, taking on the shape of an ugly, monstrous, cat-like creature. Rachel began dreaming about seeing these monstrous faces in the leaves of the trees. And she continues to have those dreams, not every night, but still too often, and she wakes up screaming at times."

"You know, I talked with Annaliese last winter, and she told me a bit about some nightmares her little boy was having. She said Theodore's nightmares centered on the bullying he was getting from a group of local Italian boys . . . a *gang*, if you will. It seems apparent that the nightmares of your niece began after witnessing that terrible accident. Such a traumatic experience poses a problem that, I think, can only be resolved with a traumatic solution. I think your niece should see a psychiatrist, Rebecca, as soon as the arrangements can be made. And I will help in any way I can."

"Oh, that's very kind of you, Madame Mitzi. My sister was reluctant to take my niece to see a psychiatrist, but since the nightmares still come more often than not, I think she will follow through with having Rachel see such a doctor. I'll let her know of your concern and your willingness to help us."

"Absolutely, Rebecca. Keep in touch with me on this. Now, ladies, lunchtime is up I'm afraid; let's get back to the shop. And thank you again for having me join you for lunch."

"You're most welcome, Madame Mitzi. The pleasure is ours. Rebecca and I enjoyed your company, immensely. Isn't that so, Rebecca?"

"Oh, absolutely, Lilly Ann. My mind was kind of out in space there for a minute. Thank you for coming, Madame Mitzi, and I will definitely speak with my sister and keep you informed."

"Sounds good, ladies. Enjoyed talking with you both. We had a great lunchtime together. We'll have to do it again sometime."

\* \* \* \*

"Lilly Ann, did you notice?"

"Notice what, Rebecca?"

"Madame Mitzi didn't seem bothered at all by the discussion of my niece's nightmares. You had been concerned that her train accident might have made her a bit squeamish when discussing such things. You remember, don't you?"

"Yes, Rebecca, I remember. But I sense there was something else weighing more heavily on Madame Mitzi's mind. It seemed to me that she swiftly moved to a conclusion regarding your niece, offered to help, and then—lunchtime was up."

"You don't think she's going to help my niece, Lilly Ann?"

"No, no, no, Rebecca. That's not what I'm saying. Of course, she will help. Madame Mitzi will keep her word. She is going to do everything she can to help your niece. But I sense there is a burden on her shoulders that involves the millinery shop. I believe she will share that burden with all of us at the big employee meeting she plans to hold. We'll have to wait and see."

\* \* \* \*

"Thank you all for coming in early today for this very important employee meeting. I have some developments to pass on to you that directly affect what we do here at our millinery shop. And some of you may not like the changes that we have to make. But make them we must. So, this will be a good time to voice your opinions after I've finished saying what I have to say. And then we can — yes, Lilly Ann, I see your hand. If you want to say something, then please, go ahead. But keep it brief, very brief."

"Madame Mitzi, I just want you to know that we are with you all the way, come what may — period!"

"Well, thank you, Lilly Ann. Judging from the nodding of everyone's heads, it looks like you've spoken for the group. Your loyalty is very much appreciated, your loyalty to me and the millinery shop. The devotion of your time and talents have allowed this shop to become one of the most successful small businesses in the region. I personally believe that our design and creation of ladies' hats and dresses leads the state — and perhaps even the entire northeastern region — in artistry and beauty. Thanks to all of you, we are known far and wide for our creativity. That creativity is really going to be put to the test now, and I will need your loyalty to really shine through, given the changes I am about to announce to you. But, some background first. Rebecca, would you reach over to that table just to your right and bring me that hat with the snowy egret feathers, with the plumes shooting upward and outward?"

"Sure. Here you go, Madame Mitzi."

"Thank you, Rebecca. Ladies, as we enter the year 1910, we have accomplished much since the days of Madame Mittón and Madame Sophie, may they both rest in peace. And as I just stated, we have achieved a great deal of success. But, for that success to continue, we must adapt to our current social environment when it comes to the making of hats for women. Our wonderfully creative hat designs that were so popular and worked in the past will no longer work now as we go forward into the future. Actually, the pressure to make changes to the design of our hats has been building for some time. It began back near the turn of the century and picked up steam under President Theodore Roosevelt. I think most of you, if not all of you, know where I'm going with this discussion. Let me draw your attention to this hat that Rebecca brought up here. These beautifully designed plumes are from the feathers of the snowy egret bird. Does anyone here know where this bird, the snowy egret, makes its home? Yes, Bërta."

"Thank you, Madame Mitzi. Although I'm fairly new to working here at the millinery shop, I am familiar with birds and how their feathers are used in the making of women's hats. I'm an avid birdwatcher, or "birder," as we are called. I have a cousin who I am very close to. He is an ornithologist who attended Cornell University, and he's a member of the Audubon Society. I've spent a great deal of time with him discussing the study of birds and going out on bird-watching trips with him. He is very well informed about birds. He knows his stuff."

"All right, Bërta, you've impressed me so far with your introduction and background on birds. I will turn the floor over to you to tell us about the snowy egret."

"Thank you, Madame Mitzi. Mind you, I am not an expert on the snowy egret, like my cousin is. But I do know a few things about that beautiful bird."

"Well, Bërta, like I said, the floor is all yours. I'll take a seat and just listen to all that you have to say. But please be mindful of the time. I need time to discuss the details of the changes we must make. And I suspect what you say is going to relate directly to what I have to say. So please, take it away."

"Yes, Madame Mitzi, thank you once again. Well, first, I think we all know and can agree that the white, light-feathery plumes of the snowy egret are quite beautiful in design and look, and because of that, they are in great demand for use in the design and creation of lady's hats. We, just like almost every other millinery shop, make extensive use of bird feathers in our hat creations, especially birds that are water fowl, like the snowy egret. As a water bird, the snowy egret lives in places like marshes, swamps, grassy ponds, ocean inlets, mangroves, and so on. They feed on fish, frogs, and other small things that thrive in and around water. The snowy egret can be found all along our lower Eastern Seaboard, from about Virginia on south, down along the Gulf Coast, also parts of the Southern California coastline, and some of the nation's warm-weather inland areas that have extensive wetlands, like around the lower Mississippi Valley leading into East Texas. The bird is quite common in Central and South America. Because of the high demand for the snowy egret's feathers, hunters thrive on killing these birds in large numbers—numbers so large that many people like my cousin are greatly disturbed by the bird's possible extinction. He criticizes me for working in a millinery shop, and I sometimes do feel a bit guilty about it. I even have dreams about seeing the faces of those birds as sort of a monstrous-like image partly hidden among the leaves of mangrove trees. The trees themselves form the image of an islet that appears to be hovering just above the water's surface, barely touching it. I get kind of scared and wake up a little frightened. I wonder, is there a message trying to be conveyed to me from somewhere out there? I don't know. But I have to earn a living, so here I am. That's about it, Madame Mitzi."

"Very good, Bërta, very good. Please ladies, give Bërta a round of applause. Thank you so much, Bërta. That is a perfect lead into what I have to say. Your knowledge of birds, and in this case, the snowy egret, is quite impressive."

"Thank you, Madame Mitzi, and to all of you, thank you."

"Give her another hand, ladies, as she takes her seat. Ladies, what you've just heard from Bërta, the alarming diminishing numbers of water birds like the snowy egret, is the reason we must stop using bird feathers in our hat creations. Matter of fact, we won't even have a supply of feathers brought to us anymore, because the killing of those birds is now considered illegal. Let's take a short fifteen-minute break and help yourselves to some treats on the table over there. We have cookies, sweet rolls, coffee, tea, and juice. So please, help yourselves to the refreshments and visit among each other. After about fifteen minutes or so, I will discuss what the social and political environment is like nowadays concerning our craft, and the ideas I have for us going forward. All right, I will see everyone back here in approximately fifteen minutes."

* * * *

"All right, ladies, may I have your attention? Please, take your seats and let's get started. Ladies! Please, we need to get started. The morning is getting away from us here. Ah, better. Thank you. Now, anyone other than Bërta can try to answer this question — Bërta, I think you'll know the answer, so please don't say anything."

"Yes, Madame Mitzi, I won't say a word. I'll keep quiet. Mum's the word."

"Okay. Have any of you ever heard the name Harriet Hemenway, and what her reputation is all about? Anyone? Speak up. Don't all raise your hands at once. Anyone care to answer? No, not you, Bërta. Don't try and meekly sneak your hand up; put it down. Like I said, I'm sure you know all about Mrs. Harriet Hemenway, so don't even think about answering just yet. I want to give someone else a try. Anyone? Come on, girls, surely someone among you besides Bërta has some knowledge or maybe heard the name of Harriet Hemenway mentioned somewhere. Anyone? All right, I'm about ready to give up on — ah, Lilly Ann, I see your hand! Go for it."

"Thank you, Madame Mitzi. I'm not sure of her reputation, but I kind of remember coming across her name."

"Good, go ahead, tell us what you know. My guess is that more of you ladies will remember her for what she has done than for what her name is. Please, Lilly Ann, the floor is yours."

"Okay, thank you again, Madame Mitzi. I'll be brief. I don't really know her background. But I do remember coming across some newspaper articles that mentioned her name. I think she had something to do with protecting birds. As a colored person, I try to keep up with news and events that are about us colored people, whether from the newspaper or simply just community gossip. What I recall is that Mrs. Harriet Hemenway was the one that invited Booker T. Washington to stay at her home when none of the hotels in Boston would rent him a room because of his race. Among us coloreds, we thought that was quite interesting and kindly thoughtful of her. Among the whites, it was just the opposite — anger and disgust over a colored man dining with a prominent white woman and her family. Anyway, that's where I know her name from, Madame Mitzi."

"Fine, very fine. Thank you, Lilly Ann. And you're right, spot on. She did have Booker T. Washington over to stay at her home and eat dinner with her and her family, I do believe. I read up on her family background a bit, and they were firmly anti-slavery —abolitionists. She kind of picked up that mantle of social justice and applied it to birds. Yes, Bërta, I see your hand. I suppose you would like to add to what Lilly Ann said, and that's fine. Just don't be too long, please."

"Thank you, Madame Mitzi. I'll try not to take up too much time. Mrs. Harriet Hemenway is one of the founders of the Audubon Society. Beginning over in Massachusetts, she, along with another lady named Minnie Hall, were appalled at the massive slaughter of birds for their feathers and stuffed bodies to adorn the tops of women's hats. They began a movement in the late 1800's against such slaughter. Their movement gained the support of our own native New York son, President Theodore Roosevelt, a conservationist and lover of birds in his own right. The politicians followed suit and passed laws that made the killing of birds, like the snowy egret, illegal. That's it. Thank you for allowing me that space, Madame Mitzi."

"That's quite all right, Bërta. Once again, a splendid job. And I see by the nodding of heads that your fellow co-workers agree, and many are now remembering Harriet Hemenway as well. Good. So, ladies, the upshot of all this is that we can no longer use bird feathers for our hats since they will no longer be supplied to us. But I will share with you what we can use. And given a little imagination coupled with your wonderful, artistic skills, I am confident our hats will continue to be second to none and the envy of the millinery industry. Lilly Ann, would you bring me that oversized satchel-bag there? Yes, that one. Thank you. All right, ladies — yes, Rebecca, you want to say something?"

"Yes. Pardon me, Madame Mitzi, but I have a question for you."

"Go right ahead; ask."

"Thank you. Are we allowed to use up the bird feathers we already have in-house, or must we discard them? And what about hats that we've already started assembling the decor for with bird feathers and stuffed birds?"

"Discard them — feathers, stuffed birds, all hats with that type of decor, discard them. I mean, here we are in late January 1910, and this must be part of the change in our operation. I don't want any controversy. I believe it is illegal to use them now, even in the trades. No, I don't want even the possibility that we might be violating the law. Best to stay away from any controversy. And speaking of controversy, we had better conclude this meeting now. It is nearly noontime and you ladies must get busy on all these standing hat orders. Otherwise, I will hear about it from the customers. Substitute some other decor or design in place of bird feathers. We'll discuss all this in more detail tomorrow at 8:00am. For now, start thinking about how to incorporate other items into the creation of a beautifully designed, artistic hat: flowers, greenery, cut glass crystals, gems, swooping curves and lines, and smaller hat dimensions, for starters. These are some of the things we'll get into. All right? Okay! Let's get to work, and I expect to see all of you in the morning at 8:00am. Now, I must step out for a bit. Lilly Ann, please oversee things until I get back."

"Yes, ma'am, I will. How long will you be gone?"

"Hopefully no more than an hour. Okay?"

"Okay, see you in an hour."

* * * *

"Good morning, Madame Mitzi."

"Good morning ladies. Please, take your seats. Thank you for being here so promptly. Before we get into our workday, I want to finish up our discussion about the changes we must make. So, let me go to my bag here. Yesterday I mentioned several items that we can use more regularly in the creation of our hats. Did any of you . . . wait a minute. As I look around, I don't see Rebecca. Lilly Ann, you and Rebecca are fairly close friends. Do you know why she's not here?"

"No, ma'am. I haven't seen or talked with her since yesterday. Perhaps she overslept and she's running a bit late this morning? I'm sure she'll be here soon. She loves working here."

"Well, I sure hope she's all right. I've heard rumors there may be another rapist about. Anyway, back to these items for hat decor. Here are some samples: a floral arrangement, costume jewelry — we could use the cut glass, especially to give that crystal-diamond look — small polished stones, ribbons, and small scarves. And here are a few sketches to show how these items might be used in our hat designs. Please, pass them around. I want everyone to take a look at them."

"These are very nice, Madame Mitzi, very creative."

"Thank you, Lilly Ann. Some of you are much more artistically gifted than I am. But all of you have an above-average talent for artistic creativity when it comes to ladies' hats; otherwise, you wouldn't be working here. Yes, Bërta?"

"Madame Mitzi, this is good. One thought I had was to maybe come up with hat designs that have a smaller brim, something light and dainty and very feminine."

"Yes, yes, that's the idea, Bërta! I was saying just yesterday that smaller dimensions with exquisitely developed lines and curves are things we need to work on. Excellent idea, Bërta. This is what I want each of you to do over the next couple of days. Sort of a homework assignment. Come up with at least three sketches of hat designs using these decorative items that we've been discussing: flowers, crystals, scarves, ribbons, and whatever else your creative minds can come up with! Yes, Coriander, I see your hand. You have a question?"

"Thank you, Madame Mitzi. Could we use artificial feathers made from some type of material that can give the realistic look of feathers?"

"Well, in principle, Coriander, that would probably be okay. But from a practical point of view, that might raise too many eyebrows among the government inspectors. Let's draw attention to our hats because of their artistic beauty rather than bringing unnecessary attention to ourselves by using artificial feathers, which may cause a stir. You follow my logic here, Coriander?"

"Yes, ma'am, I do. And that makes a lot of sense."

"Good. Now, ladies, let's get to our work benches for the day, and I'd like to see your sketches, say, by next Monday? That gives you the weekend to work on them. All right? Okay, let's hop to it and get those hat orders done. Lilly Ann, may I speak to you for a moment?"

"Yes, ma'am. Those are great ideas for our new hat designs. I think they will become quite fashionable."

"Yes, for sure. Thank you, Lilly Ann. But right now, I'm worried about Rebecca. This is not like her to miss work like this. I sure hope no one has done her any harm. I recall that she was very concerned about her niece and those nightmares. Maybe there are some family issues she's dealing with, or maybe she's sick. Anyway, after work today, would you go check on her for me, find out how she's doing and get back to me? You can take off a little early to do that. Do you mind?"

"Oh, no, not at all. I don't mind. I'm quite concerned myself. I'll go by her house, see how she's doing, and I'll get back to you."

"Thank you, Lilly Ann. Thank you very much. I appreciate it."

* * * *

"Rebecca! Here I plan to go to your house in the morning to check on you, and here you are standing on my front porch in the middle of the night. Where have you been? You have us all worried.

What are you doing here? We've been wondering where you've been!"

"Lilly Ann, may I come in? You're the only person I can come to at a time like this."

"Of course. Sure, sure, come on in. What are you doing out at this time of night? I mean, it's after midnight! Like I said, I was going to come by your place and look in on you in the morning since you didn't come to work. Madame Mitzi is very worried about you."

"Yes, I'm sure she is. And I'm sorry. But something has happened, something very strange and horrifying. Will you come with me to my sister's house? She doesn't live too far. Please, Lilly Ann, will you come? If ever we needed a friend, it's now."

"Of course, Rebecca! I'll come. I don't like leaving the kids like this, though. They're asleep. Soteria is here, of course, and I think she can look after them. But she's asleep too."

"No, Lilly Ann. There she is, right behind you, staring at us. What an odd cat, looking at us like that, like she's studying us."

"Oh, she's all right, Rebecca. Come here my, little Soteria, come here . . . that's it, Mummy is right here. You see after the kids and watch over our household while I'm out. I'll be right back in a short while. I love you, my little pet. Let Mummy give you a big kiss on the top of your furry little head. There, isn't that better? All right, Rebecca, let me grab my coat and we can go."

"I must say again, Lilly Ann, that is a very interesting and peculiar cat. She carries herself differently than any other cat I've ever seen. Most unique, almost unnatural for a cat to be so . . . to be so *attentive*, so human-like."

"Yes, yes, yes, Rebecca, she's a good pet. I've got my coat on. Let's get going. Tell me what's going on with your sister? And don't walk too fast and run off and leave me."

"Okay. Here, Lilly Ann, let's cut through here; this way. It's a quicker way to get to her house. It won't take long if we continue to walk fast, like we're doing now. I won't run off."

"Thank you, Rebecca. Now, tell me, what's going on?"

"It's Rachel, my sister's daughter. She's disappeared, or ran off, or *something*! We're not sure what to make of it. She's just *gone*, like vanished into thin air. My sister saw her to bed. Then a couple hours later, she heard some noise upstairs, like the sound of rustling leaves, she said. Very unusual. She heard what she thought was a little screech from Rachel. My sister's bedroom is downstairs from Rachel's. So, she ran upstairs to Rachel's bedroom, and *no Rachel*. My sister is absolutely beside herself. None of this makes any sense, Lilly Ann."

"Did she go to another relative's home, or maybe to her father's place?"

"No, she can't leave the house coming down those stairs without my sister hearing her. Shiphrah's bedroom is just a few feet away from the stairwell, and my sister is a light sleeper. She would definitely hear Rachel leaving if that was the case—but it wasn't! And Rachel's dad hasn't been around for years. He ran off with some other woman. It is not like Rachel to just up and leave her mother's side. I mean, my sister, Shiphrah, and Rachel are very close, extremely close. There's just too much love in that house for Rachel to just up and leave like this, especially without warning or saying something to her mother. Rachel is just not that way."

"So Shiphrah has absolutely no idea why her daughter would leave?"

"No, there is no logical explanation for Rachel's absence. None."

"Could she have been kidnapped?"

"No, I don't see how that's even possible. Shiphrah put Rachel to bed this evening. Rachel sleeps upstairs. The only way into her room is through her bedroom door. There *is* a window facing the back yard, but it's way too high for anyone to reach without a ladder — and a very tall ladder, at that. But there's no evidence of a ladder. However, I do want to show you something very strange in the back yard when we get there, before we go inside the house."

"Okay. Did your sister notify the police?"

"One of her neighbors, a gentleman named George I believe, has gone to get them. He's a real nice guy. Well, here we are, Lilly Ann. I see there are several people here now, including the police. But come around back first and tell me what you think after seeing what I'm about to show you."

"Goodness, Rebecca, you sound so . . . so mysterious."

"Well, this *is* a mystery. Come, look there: *the leaves*."

"Yes, I see the leaves on the ground. What of it? That's not unusual. Leaves are either going to be on a tree or on the ground."

"No, *look*, Lilly Ann! Look at how they lie on the ground!"

"Oh. Yes, now I see what you mean. They have formed a line or pathway, straight from that tree over there right up to the side of the house. And, mercy me, those leaves are sticking to the side of the house and trailing straight up to that window! Is that Rachel's bedroom window?"

"Yes! Yes, Lilly Ann, that is Rachel's bedroom window — *closed*. It had been locked shut from the inside and had not been opened. Come on, let's go inside. I hear my sister bawling."

"Yes, I hear her too. Sounds like she needs comforting."

"Hi, Shiphrah, I'm here. And look, I brought Lilly Ann with me."

"Uh, hi, Lilly Ann. You'll have to excuse me. Oh God, my baby, my poor baby! Where is she? Where could she possibly be?!"

"Come on, Lilly Ann, let me take you upstairs. My sister is in no shape to talk, really. I hear people up there, probably more neighbors and maybe the police. It is very strange, Lilly Ann, very strange indeed."

"Okay, Rebecca, lead the way. I'm right behind you."

"Pardon us, gentlemen, pardon us. I'm the girl's aunt and this is my good friend, Lilly Ann. I want her to see Rachel's bedroom."

"Sure, Rebecca, I know who you are. I'm George, and this here is Russell, and this gentleman is Pete. The police aren't actually here yet, but they are on their way and will probably want to open this investigation up as a Missing Child case. Meantime, we will round up more men to form a search party and go lookin' for little Rachel. She can't be too far."

"Thank you, George. I want my friend here to see Rachel's room, especially the floor. Come on in over here, Lilly Ann. Take a look and tell me what you think."

"All right, Rebecca, all right. Let me see here, let me see . . . oh my goodness! Good Lord! How . . . how can this be?!"

"You see the leaves, Lilly Ann, all over the floor? You see the leaves? A straight line on the wall underneath the bedroom window? They lead right down to the floor and then they spread out, leaves all over the floor. You see? You see, Lilly Ann? And look: leaves covering Rachel's bed. How did they get there? Where's Rachel? And look, Lilly Ann, look closely at the leaves on the floor. Look at them. Do you see it? Do you see it?"

"Calm down a bit, Rebecca. I'm looking, I'm looking as best I can. I see everything you were pointing at, and I don't have any answers. I can't even begin to explain this phenomenon. How did the leaves, so many leaves, how did they even get in here with the window closed and locked from the inside? Right?"

"Yes, Lilly Ann, the window was never opened because the lock is secured in place. Rachel can't unlock it; Shiphrah has to do it. The sobbing and wailing of my sister is bothering me, Lilly Ann. I'm going to have to go downstairs and try to comfort her. But before I go, look again at the leaves on the floor, Lilly Ann, look very closely. Do you see what I see? What all of us see?"

"Well, I can't say that I do just yet. But let me walk around to this side and take a . . . take a look and . . . Oh, my God! There's a face! There's a face that has formed in the leaves! And it looks like an animal's face, a hideous-looking animal that favors a wild cat, so it appears to me."

"Yes, Lilly Ann, the image of a strange-looking feline. A horror-looking monstrosity, very strange, very peculiar. It reminds me of your cat, Lilly Ann. This face in the leaves is more grotesque, more altered, but doggone it, I see a rough impression of your cat—Soteria!"

"Rebecca! You see Soteria in the face of those leaves? Really? Soteria? *Soteria?!*"

*Musical Box*

# THE MUSIC BOX

*My thoughts are in a whirl, a dizzying, puzzling whirl. Where did this music box come from? Who left it at the front door of my apartment? And why the picture of a dancing woman surrounded by dancing cats standing on their hind legs? I better ask some of the neighbors and see if they saw who left it here. It had to be left here by mistake. This belongs to someone else. I can't hang around to figure this out right now. I've got to get to work this morning, down at the millinery shop. I'll bring the box inside and put it on the coffee table. I'll have to ask the neighbors about it when I get home from work. I must get walking to work now. It's a pretty music box, though. Lots of fine wood and polished metal. I don't have the time to listen to what music it plays. I'll listen to it later. I must go. I've got to get down to the shop. The music box can wait.*

\* \* \* \*

"Good morning, Madame Mitzi."

"Good morning, ladies. Please, take your seats. I want to first say that I think we are going to have a great year in this year of 1910! So many events and occasions will be coming our way, from political events, to sporting events, to social activities, that will lead to greater demand for our hats! We are going to get very busy and — yes, Lilly Ann."

"Thank you, Madame Mitzi. I just wanted to mention the NAACP will be having their second annual convention in New York City, right at the end of May. We colored women love wearing our hats. So that convention could be a great source for hat sales."

"Lilly Ann! No no, it's Rebecca. I'm behind you, way in the back near the wall. What do the letters N-A-A-C-P mean?"

"Oh, there you are! It stands for National Association for the Advancement of Colored People. It started last year, in 1909, by Mr. Dubois and several others, including some white people. Their purpose is to help colored people fight against segregation, discrimination, lynching, working without pay because of some bogus debt claimed by an employer, and advocate for our basic civil rights and all that goes with them. And by the way, Mr. Dubois is a very fine poet and writer. I read some of his work whenever I can."

"Oh, wow, that's great, Lilly Ann! Thanks for sharing. Would I be allowed to join the NAACP even though I'm not colored? I'm a white Jewish girl."

"Of course, Rebecca, of course you can get involved and join the NAACP. Matter of fact, with you being Jewish, your people have also experienced your share of animosity from others over the centuries, simply because you are Jewish."

"All right, girls, time to stop the chit-chat. Let's get to work on those hat and dress orders. But before you dive into your work, I have this proposal for you: There have been a number of new faces that have come on board within the past year, like Bërta here. I'd like us all to get to know each other a little better. I certainly would like to know all of you a little better, and that includes reconnecting with those of you that have been here for several years, like Rebecca. I'd like to meet with you in small groups of, say, three at a time, after work when your after-work schedules, activities, and home life allow. I'll work my way around to each of you."

"That is a wonderful idea, Madame Mitzi, simply wonderful!"

"Thank you, Lilly Ann. Okay! That's it! Thank you for being so attentive. Now, everyone back to work. Uh, Lilly Ann, let me speak to you for just a minute."

"Sure, Madame Mitzi. Is everything all right?"

"Yes, yes, everything is fine. For my first small group meeting, I'd like to start with you, Rebecca, and Bërta. Is that okay with you?"

"Of course, Madame Mitzi, you don't even have to ask. I am totally and completely devoted to you and the millinery shop."

"Thank you, dear. Your loyalty is greatly appreciated. I suspect there are some I've hired who may have intentions of undermining our shop for the benefit of some competitor. But enough about that. I'll share my thoughts with you some other time on that subject. But for now, would you go get Rebecca and Bërta, and let's meet briefly in my office. I'd like to see if we four can schedule a date after work where we can socialize a bit and learn a bit more about each other. And this would really be for the benefit of Bërta, since you, Rebecca, and myself have known each for the better part of ten years. Okay?"

"Yes, ma'am, for sure. I'll go get them right now."

"Great. Thank you, Lilly Ann,"

\* \* \* \*

"Thanks, girls, for arranging your home schedules for us to spend this time together. And what a beautiful spring day it is, a lovely Saturday on this 28th day of May 1910! The weather is just lovely, a nice, warm, late afternoon."

"It's our pleasure to spend this time with you, Madame Mitzi. All three of us have been looking forward to this get together."

"Well, thank you, Lilly Ann. I thought it would be good to start with you ladies. And this is primarily for the benefit of you, Bërta, in that I know Lilly Ann and Rebecca fairly well. They've been good workers at the millinery shop for some time now. How long has it been, Rebecca? You and Lilly Ann have been here about ten years?"

"Yes, ma'am, that's about right, give or take a few."

"If I may say, Madame Mitzi, I am absolutely delighted to be here with you, Lilly Ann, and Rebecca for socializing time, since we all work together. I think this is very positive."

"I agree. For starters, if I may, Madame Mitzi?"

"Sure, Lilly Ann, go right ahead."

"I think it would be great if we start by sharing a little bit about our backgrounds, families, and the experiences that led us to come work at the millinery shop."

"Wonderful, Lilly Ann! And please allow me to be first, since I'm the new kid on the block, so to speak, and the least known among you all. Is that okay, Madame Mitzi?"

"By all means, Bërta, the floor is yours. We'll just sip on our beverages, eat our refreshments, and listen to you tell us all about yourself. Please, go ahead."

"Thank you, Madame Mitzi. Let me first say that I am of German heritage."

"Oh! Kind of like Annaliese, who used to work with us. She's from Germany."

"Yes, Rebecca, I saw her when she came to visit the shop a while back. We didn't get to meet, but she seemed like a nice person. Those that knew her were glad to see her."

"She is a very nice and beautiful person, Bërta. I'm sure you would have liked her if you'd had the opportunity to meet her. Her husband is one handsome man, too! Tall, dark-skinned — he's a Negro — and he loves Annaliese dearly. They have a cute little boy, too, named after President Roosevelt."

"Oh, that sounds lovely, Madame Mitzi. Let me clarify. Although I'm of German heritage, I was not born in Germany. I was born here in the United States, right here in New York. My grandparents came to America and brought my mother when she was a young girl of about twelve or thirteen years old. She was an only child. When mother was about seventeen years old, her father, my grandfather, died from cancer. Grandmother did not last too long after that. I'd say probably within three years or so, she contracted tuberculous and died shortly thereafter. I don't remember my grandfather, but I did know my grandmother. I was about three or four when she died. I can say that after Grandmother's death, my mother changed, and things kind of got rough for us, my mother and me."

"Wait a minute, Bërta, if I may ask; where was your father? Wasn't he around?"

"No, I'm sorry to say, Lilly Ann, that I never knew my father. My mother became pregnant with me at around age sixteen, maybe a little younger. Anyway, he didn't want to marry her or help her take care of me, so he left. Mother never saw him again."

"Men! Some, if not most men, can be such scoundrels, it makes me sick! They seem to only want what they can get between a woman's legs, and once they have it, they dump her like she has the plague."

"Believe it or not, Lilly Ann, you are not far from the truth, at least in my mother's case. You see, from about age five until I was a teenager, I was raised in and around New York City's brothels."

"My goodness, Bërta. Your life as a child must have been quite interesting, to say the least."

"Yes, it was, Madame Mitzi. I was born November 10, 1887, in Little Germany in Manhattan. I remember being told that was a Thursday. My grandmother nurtured me while my mother went to work as a seamstress. Her hours were long and hard, but it was an honest, decent job. Thank goodness for my grandmother. When Grandmother died, Mother said that we could no longer continue living on the wages of a lowly seamstress. So, she turned to an occupation in which she could watch over me and not have to pay someone else while, at the same time, make more money than she did sewing. She became, what I call, a professional in the sex trade. She became a prostitute."

"Bërta! Bërta, wait, stop right there. You don't have to go into that side of your family life if you don't want to. I imagine it could be quite embarrassing, and maybe even emotionally painful for you to —"

"No, Madame Mitzi, it's all right. I feel fine sharing my history with you and Lilly Ann and Rebecca. It's good to remember, and to remind oneself from whence one came, to borrow a phrase from the Bible."

"Yes, Bërta, that phrase occurs many times in our *Torah* as well. Our Shabbat, which began Friday at sunset, concluded earlier today. And the concept of remembrance is frequently mentioned in our Torah teaching."

"Yes, Rebecca, I'm sure it does."

"Well, Bërta, if that's the case, then you've got me anxious to hear the rest of your story. Please, do continue."

"Thank you, Lilly Ann. I don't want to drag this out for too long, if I can help it. I'll do my best to fill in some details. Like I said, our family first lived in Little Germany, which was over on the Lower East Side of

Manhattan. I don't remember that neighborhood. But what I do remember is that after Grandmother died and Mother entered the profession, we lived in a place called the Music Box, located on Mulberry Bend in the Five Points neighborhood of Lower Manhattan. It was like a hotel with five floors, with maybe a dozen small rooms on each floor. The rooms were only equipped with a bed, sink, toilet, a few wash towels, and a garment stand to hang clothes. That was it. The rooms were rented out to customers at an hourly rate for their entertainment and, ultimately, sexual activity. Our living quarters was on the top floor. The only difference from the other floors is that we had a commonly shared kitchen area on our floor. Several other women, some with children, lived there too. That's where I grew up. And I hated it, except for maybe one thing."

"You mean there was something you liked in that kind of environment, Bërta?"

"Well, Lilly Ann, the one thing I admired about that place was the decor. It was absolutely fabulous. No, I didn't like all the promiscuity and drunkenness, with all kinds of people engaging in these wild and noisy, disgusting orgies, but the decorations and furnishings were first-class. I mean, there were figurines and statues replicating Italian and Greek sculptures, beautifully designed Persian rugs with striking colors, rich-looking rosewood furniture, huge mirrors, gas lamps, and flower vases that looked like they came from an expensive museum. I mean, that receiving room, which was fairly large, and the paintings that decorated the walls throughout the building, were something to behold. For men, the decor definitely set the tone for pleasurable sexual enjoyment."

"Goodness, Bërta, it sounds like the kind of decorations only the wealthy could afford."

"That's about right, Rebecca. But like I said, I hated living there, so I moved out after I turned eighteen. I learned to sew from my mother and I, like my mother, went to work as a seamstress. It was a sweat shop, but that's where I also learned how to make ladies' hats, kind of on the side. A fellow worker there showed me, in her spare time and during our breaks, how to design and put a hat together. After making up a few hats myself, I found that I had a knack for it and really enjoyed making these hats for women. After Mother died in 1908, I decided to leave the city and look for work as a lady's hat maker. Finally, last year, I heard about the Millinery Shop in Schuylerville and decided to go there and look for work making women's hats. Madame Mitzi hired me. So here I am. That's about it."

"And I have no regrets whatsoever in hiring you, Bërta. You are a wonderful employee, very talented and creative. Comes from your good German background, I presume."

"Thank you, Madame Mitzi. That's very nice of you to say as much. I don't know if I deserve too much of that. But that's my story."

"Nonsense! You deserve every compliment you get, and then some! Especially given the environment you were raised in."

"Wait a minute, Bërta, not so fast. I don't know about Madame Mitzi, but Rebecca and I want to hear more about that environment you were raised in, don't we, Rebecca?"

"Yes, for sure. Lilly Ann's right, Bërta, I do want to hear more. But first, let me share with you ladies what I found outside my apartment door the other morning. Somebody placed a beautifully ornate, wooden music box right at my door. There was no note, no message, no nothing, just the music box."

"Was it intended for one of your neighbors and left accidentally at your door, Rebecca?"

"No, Bërta, I asked all the neighbors. No one was expecting a delivery of a music box. I also checked with the lost and found at our police precinct station, and no music box has been reported missing or stolen."

"Have you listened to the tune it plays?"

"A little bit, Lilly Ann, just a little bit. It's a tune played on a piano. I'm not totally familiar with it, but it does sound kind of familiar. It reminds me of a tune that a band would play, sort of like what was playing when everyone was celebrating President Teddy Roosevelt's election victories."

"Oh! That probably was "Hot Time in the Old Town Tonight"! It's also popular in saloons, dance halls, and theaters."

"You know, you're probably right, Madame Mitzi. Along with that tune, inside the box and on the underside of the lid was a drawing of a woman scantily dressed, standing on one leg as if she is dancing.

Surrounding her in a circle are five cats that stand on their hind legs and pose as if they are dancing around the woman."

"I'd like to see that music box, Rebecca. I think we all would."

"I agree with you, Lilly Ann. That description kind of reminds me of what I've seen at the Music Box brothel."

"That makes it even more interesting to hear the rest of your story, Bërta."

"Sure, Lilly Ann. Let me see, where should I pick it back up? I can tell you some of what I remember of when my mother was working there at the Music Box. Although I'd rather leave out some of the seedy, disgusting behavior of the male customers and those women, including my mother. I don't think her heart was ever really in it — she simply needed the money. And mother made a lot of money working at the Music Box. The owner of the building and madam of the brothel was a lady named Madame Leonine. She promoted her business using a cat theme. She got the idea, so I was told, from ancient Egypt. They worshipped this cat-goddess as a protector of their households. She had the body of a woman, but the head of a cat. So anyway, Madame Leonine had girls of different races and nationalities. There was Colored, White, Asian, Indian, all with different skin tones from very light to very dark. They would dress up in these skimpy dresses with cat images on them. These girls, in their cat outfits, would perform for the gentlemen in the main banquet hall. Her saloon hall had these colorful paintings of women, mostly half-naked, on the walls all the way around. I have to admit that I did have one favorite painting. It was of a woman with very light, off-white skin color. She was naked from her hips up. The garment around her hips, which was very colorful, was just above her pubic hairline. The garment was painted in such a way as to make it look like it was falling. She was in a striking dance pose, bare footed, with her breasts protruding and her hips conveying a swaying motion. Her arms were raised, and her hands were placed together, just above her head. A cluster of small jewels were set in her hair, with long, beautiful, jewel earrings in her ear lobes and matching bracelets stacked around her wrists. She was being waited on by an attractive olive-skinned woman on one side, like someone from the Middle East, and a very beautiful black African woman in colorful clothing on the other side. Presumably, both servants were slaves. It was a very striking painting. After the public entertainment, the men and women would generally pair off and go to a room for some private entertainment and sex. If a man had enough money, he would have two or more women, um, *entertain* him. There was always sex going on, around the clock. The girls worked in shifts, and the men just kept coming, nonstop, from all walks of life, rich and poor alike. They all needed their sporting thrill to relieve the stress of their jobs and home life. At least that's how it was explained to me . . . a justifiable necessity for the overall good and welfare of society. That's it, ladies. That was the environment I was brought up in, and I hated every minute of it. The smelly mixture of perfume, men's body odors, and alcohol was nauseating. I hated it."

"Well, Bërta, your mother did what she felt she had to do in order to survive. Did you have any brothers or sisters?"

"No, Madame Mitzi, I was her only child."

"May I ask you one more question, Bërta?"

"Sure, Rebecca, ask away."

"You said that the Egyptian cat-goddess was a protector of households, right?"

"Yes, that's right."

"Well, uh, Lilly Ann, isn't that what you say about your cat, Satire? That she's a protector for you and your children?"

"Her name is *Soteria*, Rebecca, and she *is* our protector, and a darn good one too. None like her. I don't know what you're driving at, Rebecca, but I think I need to say two things. One: Soteria was not around five-thousand years ago when Egypt ruled the world. And two: she's from Louisiana, not Egypt!"

"Granted. But her ancestors could have come from Egypt, Lilly Ann. Yours is a very odd cat, and she even looks strange, like that horrid cat-face that was in the leaves on the floor of my niece's bedroom. And my niece is still missing! Nobody can find her. No one knows where she is or what she could be doing. It's a mystery, and it's awful, just awful."

"Rebecca, I'm sorry that your niece is missing. But I can tell you what she is *not* doing. She is not blaming a house cat for her kidnapping. Why get on my cat? What do you know about cats? Do you own one?"

"No, I don't own a cat, Lilly Ann. But if I did, I would not want a cat like that disgusting fleabag at your house!"

"Why, you lying hypocrite! At my house, where we fed you and made you feel welcomed as a good friend, you said you *wanted* a cat like Soteria! You seemed to express nothing but admiration for her! All the good things you said were they just lies, Rebecca? Were you lying to me the whole time you were at my house, Rebecca?"

"No, I wasn't lying, Lilly Ann! But that was then, *before* my niece disappeared and that image of a ferocious-looking cat appeared in that pile of leaves on her bedroom floor—an image strikingly similar to your cat! And now my darling niece, Rachel, is nowhere to be found! It just makes me sick. Sick!"

"So, you're blaming my cat, Soteria, for the disappearance of your niece? How stupidly ridiculous that all sounds! You are talking like a raving lunatic, Rebecca! How can a cat take off with your niece, for God's sake?"

"Well, how do you explain that cat-face in the leaves then, huh? And given what Bërta just said about the mystics of Egypt worshipping cats because of their so-called gifts of protection, and what you say about the protection that your cat provides, it all seems to connect to me, as crazy as it sounds, it all just seems to connect!"

"Rebecca! Rebecca, listen to yourself! You sound like a ..."

"Girls! Girls! Please, let's stop the arguing! I'm tired, and I'm sure Bërta is tired. And it seems obvious that you two need to go to your respective homes and cool off. Lilly Ann?"

"Yes, Madame Mitzi, you're right. We need to calm down and go home."

"Rebecca?"

"Yes, Madame Mitzi, I agree. Time to go and cool down."

"Bërta, you okay?"

"Yes, Madame Mitzi. I didn't mean to cause such a stir. Maybe I said too much. I'm sorry."

"Nonsense, Bërta. Your story was great, and you are inspiring for how you came out of that awful environment and found yourself employed in a wonderful, and legal, occupation. No need to apologize. You did fine."

"Thank you, Madame Mitzi. And thanks to both of you, Lilly Ann and Rebecca, for listening."

"Great. Now, Lilly Ann, Rebecca, Bërta, each of you go home, get a good night's rest, and have a pleasant Sunday tomorrow. I trust I will see each of you on Monday back at the shop, getting along and ready to put in a good day's work. Goodbye."

\* \* \* \*

*All right, let me get in this apartment and examine that music box. Where is my door key? Come on, Rebecca, think! Where did I put that key? Ah! Here it is.*

*Okay, now where did I place that music box? It's not in the living room, nor the kitchen. I know I left it on this coffee table. I left it right here. I'm positive! I always keep it right here. I never move it. But it has been moved. Blast it, where is that music box? Am I losing my mind? Maybe Lilly Ann was right about me. Maybe my mind is going haywire. I think maybe it's the stress of not knowing where Rachel is. This is so upsetting. Oh well, that box has got to be around here somewhere. I might as well go into the bedroom and change clothes. And maybe it will—ah, there it is! I must have moved it from the coffee table to the bedroom. But it's sitting on the bed. I couldn't have placed it on my bed. But yet, there it is on my bed. There couldn't have been anyone else in here. Or could there? Well, I'll set this thing on the nightstand and examine it from there. Let's see, I'll just open this lid, turn this key, and . . . hmm, that tune, now I do remember it. President Roosevelt had it played, something about hot time tonight in the town, I think. Wow! All of a sudden, I feel so sleepy. I'll close the lid, lay down, and grab me a short nap. Goodness, my eyes are so heavy with sleepiness. Where did this drowsiness come from? Oh, good. It feels good to lay down, and . . . and . . . what is that light coming from the music box? I know I just closed that lid. I know I did. How is it that the lid is now open? How did that music come on by itself? God, it's getting so bright. And I am so sleepy, sooo sleepy, so . . .*

\*\*\*\*

"Anyone seen Rebecca? Lilly Ann?"

"No, Madame Mitzi. I've gone by her place several times, but there's no answer. I don't know where she is or where she could be. Her sister, Shiphrah, hasn't seen her either. Nor have Rebecca's neighbors, at least those I talked to. Her sister is quite worried, and she did make a missing person's report with the police."

"Thank you, Lilly Ann. This is really strange. First Rebecca's niece goes missing under the most unusual of circumstances, and now Rebecca is also missing with no plausible explanation. Perhaps we should cut this workday short and join the hunt for Rebecca, and maybe go and visit with her sister. I bet she is quite distraught, missing her daughter and now her sister."

"Madame Mitzi."

"Yes, Bërta."

"Did anyone, like the police or Rebecca's sister, come across that music box of hers that she'd talked about?"

"No, there has been no mention of a music box. Rebecca was so distraught over her missing niece; I wonder if it was all just a delusion in her mind? Well, let's call it a day, ladies. See you tomorrow morning. Tomorrow would be Tuesday, right? Oh yes, now I'm allowing myself to get all mixed up! Let's remember Rebecca and her family in our prayers, if you'd be so inclined. Have a good day."

"Lilly Ann, may I walk part way home with you? I live in the same direction you're going. I've seen you walk this way before, and I think you're a little further down from where I live. Is that okay?"

"Of course, Coriander. Sure, we can talk a bit as we walk along. What's on your mind?"

"I'm still fairly new here at the millinery shop, and I'm beginning to wonder how stable it is, given all this talk I hear about cats, and music boxes, and faces in leaves, and people coming up missing. It's all kind of unnerving, you know?"

"Don't pay too much attention to all that, Coriander. Most of it is due to stress, particularly since we can't make ladies' hats the way we use to. Birds and their feathers are against the law now. So, we've had to come up with new and creative ideas for hats. All this will soon pass. You'll see. Everything will be back to normal."

"I sure hope so. Well, this is where I make my turn toward my place. Thanks for the talk, Lilly Ann."

"Sure, no problem, Coriander. Have a good evening."

* * * *

*Now calm yourself, Coriander. Here I go, talking to myself, as usual. But Lilly Ann's words were comforting. I wish I was more comfortable climbing these four flights of stairs up to my apartment. Once my money gets better, I think I'll look for a place on the ground level or first floor. But no higher. It is becoming too hard for me to trudge up these steps. And they seem to get higher and higher. Well, here we are at my door, and what's this I see? It's some sort of a box. A wooden box. Let's see. Oh, a music box! What's this picture here under the lid? For heaven's sake, that's a woman standing there, practically naked. Her breasts are showing. She has some sort of a loose-fitting cloth around her hips, just below her navel. What are those tiny figures that have formed a circle around her? Let me get inside my apartment under better light, where I can get a closer look and see what it is they're doing, and . . .why, they're men kneeling! They are kneeling and facing toward that half-naked female figure, as if they're worshipping her! Let me get a better look at her. I can't quite make it out, my eyes might be playing tricks on me, and . . . and . . . Jesus, Mary and Joseph, she has the head of a cat!*

*Villares Barbosa ~ Study of Female Nude*

# DISTORTIONS

*Who am I? Who am I? I don't know. I cannot remember. I cannot remember. Let me think, but my thoughts are all confused. Try, remember! I can't. Thoughts twisted, fuddled, puzzled. Why can't I remember? So many questions. So few answers. Who am I? Who am I? What am I? What am I? Wait! Yes, I remember, and I see, I am a woman. A nice woman. But who am I? Thoughts . . . distorted . . .*

*Where am I? This room, how did I get here? Where did I live? Somewhere, somewhere, but where? Was it New York? Was it New York? Why New York? Why does New York come to mind? A place in New York, maybe? But what place? Some place, right? Some town, some city. But where? Am I there? Did I never leave? Thoughts confused, puzzled, twisted . . . distorted . . .*

*What did I do? What was my job? Money, how did I make my money? Where did I work? Was it from hats? The hats, the hats. Why do hats suddenly come to mind? Wait, ladies' hats, right? I created ladies' hats, right? But why hats? Popular, fashionable, feminine. But no hats here in this room. Why not? Thoughts all confused, twisted, puzzled . . . distorted . . .*

*This wall. Nothing but this brick wall and this stool I sit on and a small book case . . . with nothing in it. And I have nothing on. I'm naked. Why am I naked? Do I like being naked? I don't know. Where are the answers? Why am I naked? Why am I in this room? My thoughts, so confused, twisted, puzzling . . . distorted . . .*

*What brought me here? The cat. Why does the cat come to mind? I can't remember, but there is a cat. But why? And leaves, why am I thinking about leaves? Is there something in the leaves? What could that be? Perhaps the cat was in the leaves? Wait, that's right, the cat was in the leaves. But why? And how could a cat bring me into this room? How did I get here? Was it by carriage? Or by train? A train, a train. I seem to recall. Yes, I remember now. There was a train, but it got into a wreck. And she was killed. But who is she? She had something to do with the hats, maybe? I just can't remember. So many questions. So few answers. Thoughts confused, puzzled, twisted . . . distorted . . .*

*But there was a box, right? Yes, a box! But what type of box? Wait, wait, I remember. It was a music box. But why a music box? What tune did it play? I don't remember, I just don't remember. And what was inside the music box. Think, think, think hard.*

*What was inside that music box? I can't, I can't remember. I just can't remember. I don't think I liked it, whatever it was. Or did I? But wait, am I getting a picture of what was inside? Is something coming into focus inside my mind here while I ponder on these thoughts? Maybe, maybe. A woman, naked, yes, totally naked, like I am now. I know I am naked, but why am I naked? Where did this room come from? There's not much in here. Only this wall, a stool, and a little empty bookcase. But where did they come from? I don't even know where I am or how I got here. So confusing, twisted, puzzling that my thoughts are so crazy . . . distorted . . .*

*This building. I hear noises. Noises, what sort of noises? Groaning? Is that groaning noises I hear? Is it pain? Or pleasure? I hear voices, lots of voices. Whose voices are they? Men's voices? Women's voices? And music, barely, I can hear, very faint. But I hear music. What kind of music? The voices, they are laughing, men and women together, they are laughing. But why? Is there a theater, a comedy, a stage acting? What could it be that is causing such noise, such a ruckus? Now singing. Do I hear singing? Yes, that must be singing. Whoever they are, they are certainly having a good time, some sort of celebration. But what could they be celebrating? Birthday? Holiday? Special occasion? What could it be? Maybe a marriage? If so, who got married? Maybe I know them. But if I did know them, how come I am not out there with them, joining in the celebration? Maybe I wasn't invited. All that noise down there. Yes, down there. So I guess I must be upstairs somewhere, right? Somewhere upstairs in this building. But what sort of building is this? What am I doing here? Thoughts confused, puzzled, twisted . . . distorted . . .*

*Oh, I hear footsteps! Loud, thudding footsteps. As if they are marching up a set of stairs. Whoever it is, maybe they will give me some answers. Maybe they will straighten out my distorted thoughts. Now I hear them, right outside, just beyond that door. Now what will happen? Who's coming in the door? Who's coming in the door?*

"All right, Rebecca, quit daydreaming and get your ass out of this room right now. You've got a couple of good-paying customers waiting to see you, and they are anxious to be entertained. And you better show them a damn good time. I want them coming back to the Music Box for more, you understand? No more of this silly talk you've been doing. No more confusion, no more questions. Give these men good sex, you got it?"

"Yes, Madame Leonine. I got it. I'm coming out right now. I will show these men a good time and give them good sex."

*Fluvial Nymph*

# THE NEREID NYMPH

*In the valley by the river where the tall grass grows, there lives a maiden without any clothes.*

*A lovely creature, tall and svelte. The hearts of men, she can definitely melt.*

*She walks with a sway, full nudity in bloom. She bathes in the river, by the night's full moon.*

*She has a dark side, nobody knows. Concealed in guile, like water it flows.*

*A beautiful maiden, a nymph as she goes. Along by the river, where the tall grass grows.*

\* \* \* \*

"Velcome home, Adam, my huzbund. Did you have a nize trip? Looked at plenty of horzez?"

"Yes, Annaliese, it was a fine trip. And yes, I looked at a number of Argentinian thoroughbreds. I think we have several potential winners for the Wheelhouse Stables. Maybe even a big derby winner or two. Uhh, did I just see a cat scamper into that room?"

"Zat is goot, Adam. I'll tell you in a moment about zee cat. But let me azk you. Did you zee many vimen, zhose Zouth American luzty femalez? Did you look zem over too, Adam? Like zee horzez you vurk out vith, did you vurk out vith zee vimen too, Adam?"

"Annaliese, please, let's not get started on that. I've got enough worries outside this house, and I certainly don't need added ones from inside this house. Look, I mind my own business when I am away. I travel to do a job for my boss, Mr. Wheelhouse. And I think I do a fine job too, and Mr. Wheelhouse certainly agrees, which is why he sends me on these trips. But my worries go beyond doing a good job. I mean, here we are at war near the end of 1917, the government has been rounding up us black men for months to serve in their segregated army.

I mean, they lynch and murder us here at home. Then send the remnants of us to Europe to get gassed and killed in France, Germany, or wherever else the hell they want to send us. Mr. Wheelhouse is trying to pull some strings, so I won't have to go. But that is still up in the air. I really don't know if he can pull it off. Then we got these two boys here, thirteen-year-old Theodore and eight-year-old Allan, that I have to keep working to bring food in this house for you and them. And then ..."

"Adam, Adam, zlow down. I'm zorry if I upzet you. Lizen, I'm not mad, upzet or even annoyed. I just vanted to know und for you to be truthful vith me. You are a hanzum man, a very hanzum man. Vimen are going to be attracted to you, und you to zem.

Ezpecially vhen you are avay from me for monthz und monthz at a time. You have feelinz' for zex vich iz natural. Und I'm not zhere. I underztand, Adam, believe me, I underztand."

"Do you, Annaliese, do you really understand?"

"Yez, Adam, I do. Vhen you are avay for zo long, I expect you to do vhat men do. All I vant iz vhen you come home to me, zat you only have eyez for me. Zat you zee und kizz only my titten. Zat you zee and feel only my arzch. Zat you zee, zmell, und fondle only my muzchi. Zat you empty your love only into me, no one elze. Iz zat okay, Adam?"

"Okay, Annaliese, I'm good with that. I do love you, very much, I really do. Come here and let me show you how much I love you."

"Umm, oooo, you bad dog! I love it. Litzen, I had a dream und I wrote zum zings down. Zhe boyz are zleep, so I vant you to read vhat I wrote. Let me get it for you."

"Alright. Uhh, where did the cat come from?"

"Oh, zat iz a gift from Lilly-Ann for zee boyz. Her cat, Zoteria, had zum kittenz vile zey vere viziting at Lilly-Ann'z family home in Louiziana."

"Oh, I see. Just what kind of cat is it? Do you know?"

"No, I don't. I'll have to azk Lilly-Ann next time I zee her. Ahh, here it iz. I zink I wrote in zee correct Englizh, about zis dream. Here, I vant you to read it. Vill you?"

"Okay, I'll read it. Aloud?"

"Yez, pleez, read it out loud."

"Alright, here goes. I do see, Annaliese, that at least you do not write with a German accent. Okay, I guess it wasn't all that funny. Let's see, I guess I should start reading right here ...

* * * *

Looks like Annaliese be let'n Adam off duh hook 'bout him seein' anut'her lady or ladies when hee's out'uh-town, 'way frum Queens, New York where dey live, like when he in Souse America. Buh wha'bout if he be out'uh-town over in New Jersey? He could be lookin' fuh horses arrivin' by boat from Souse America or wherever, righ'? I wonder if'n out'uh-town logic still apply? Or, how 'bout when he up at Sara'oga Racecourse? 'Hat racecourse is 'bout 295 kilome-'ers from Queens ... defini-'ly out'uh-town. Umm, New Jersey, Saratoga! Ahh, I'm a get'n bet'er prouncin' muh t's and losin' the accen' guv-nuh.Yuh think? I been workin' at it. There, you see.

Anyway, Adam in New Jersey. Adam at Saratoga. Adam back in New Jersey. And den back at'uh racecourse. Much water, a lot-uh water and tall grass in-nem places.

There may be sum'-um developin' here. Let's find out.

* * * *

What an odd dream I just had. I see a woman, sitting at a desk, writing something down.

"I don't see anything odd about that, Annaliese."

"Pleez, Adam, juz read. Zave the commentz for later after you've finished. Don't juzt zhrug your zhoulderz, go head, read."

I cannot make out what she is writing. It could be a letter, or a poem, or a story. A speech maybe? I just don't know. But suddenly, as dreams will do, the scene changes to an entirely different setting. There's no explanation and I can't figure out why the change. But it happened.

I'm looking at this scene of a marketplace, like a farmer's market, out in the open. It's a bright sunny day, and it actually appears to be hot. Men, I guess the farmers, are standing behind their food stands. There are fruit stands, vegetable and produce stands, with a few old people, just a handful of them, picking over the fruit and vegetables. However, there is only one meat stand. There's a colored man working the stand. But here is the odd thing. There are women, in single file, lined up in front of his meat stand.

"Ohh, Annaliese, this dream is really starting to sound interesting now. Enough about old folks pickin' over oranges or lettuce. I like…"

"Adam, pleez, remember, no commentz till you finizh. Pleez, read."

The very odd thing about these women lined up in front of the gentleman's meat stand is that they are all naked, practically. No shoes, no clothes. They are barefoot and totally, absolutely nude with but one exception. They are all wearing hats! The type of stylish hats that are made at the millinery shop where I worked for so many years.

"Annaliese, I got to stop here and say something. My goodness, woman, you really have a descriptive dream here. You actually recalled all this detail?"

"Yez, Adam, I did. Az zoon az I voke up, I immediately ztarted writing vhat I zaw in my dream. Pleez, continue. You're almozt done.

The gentleman's meat stand area is chocked full of meat, all kinds of meat. There's beef, chicken, lamb, pork, even wild game such as duck, rabbit, pheasant, and there's horse meat. There is just about every cut of meat you can imagine. Steaks, ribs, bacon, ham, leg-of-lamb, and the horse meat. It's all there, and these naked women in their hats are buying just his meats.

No fruit or produce, just his meats. They seem to be mostly focused on buying horse meat. How odd. And all the women are white. The line of women must be forty or fifty deep, all naked but wearing these attractive ladies' hats, and no one seems to care. Even the colored gentleman selling the meat does not seem moved by his naked female customers. Although I really think he is pretending not to be moved. He is certainly not blind, and all these white women are good looking to. It's odd, no colored women, just white women.

The hats they wear are beautiful, stunning, magnificent workmanship, absolutely gorgeous. With feathers, rhinestones, ribbons, some with jewels, swirls and floral, with material that looks like silk and velvet and what ever lush material one can think of. These hats could have been made at our millinery shop by Lilly-Ann, or Sophie, or Mitzi or Madame Mittón, or even me. The End.

"Wow, Annaliese, that is quite some dream. Do you recall or have any idea what the colored guy selling the meat looked like?"

"No, Adam, I can't zay zhat I do. It could have been you, or zome of your friendz, I mean it could have been any colored guy. I do find it curiouz zhat of all zee different meat he had zhere at hiz ztand, zheze naked white women in their fine hatz were moztly buying the horze meat by far. You are colored, you vork vith horzez, I am vhite and I uze to vork in a zhop makin' hatz."

"Well, there you have it, Annaliese. There's your dream. You had all those things on your mind before you went to sleep, and so you dreamt about them. Seems pretty cut-n-dry to me."

"Maybe zo, Adam, maybe zo. But I vonder. Let'z go to bed and zay goodnight."

"Goodnight, Annaliese."

\* \* \* \*

That dream Annaliese had was quite a doozy, wasn't it? I hope you can tell that I'm tryin' to speak muh English more clearly and lose 'hat Bri-ish accent. Anyway, naked white women lined up to buy horsemeat from a fully-clothed colored man! I guess there is meaning in all that or maybe not. Just a crazy dream. It would be nice if I could dream about fur-less female cats lined up to see me about whatever. They can be of any color to, I'm not prejudice, as long they are female and hot. Oh well, I can fan-uh-size, can't I?

Speakin' of fan-sizing, I believe 'his story is about to introduce a fantastical element. Judging from the dream of Annaliese relatin' tuh female nudity, horses and colored men, 'his story sounds like it is going to get really interestin' as the calendar moves from 1917 to 1918.

**101**

Well, Guv-nuh, let's read on.

\* \* \* \*

"Good morning, Annaliese. I beat you up this morning. I decided to fix myself a cup of coffee."

"Yez, you beat me up. Und a goot mornin' to you to, Adam. I'll take a cup of zhat coffee."

"Look at this newspaper headline here, a child molester and possible rapist is on the loose here in New York. When he's caught, they should shoot him right there on the spot. Why waste money on attorneys, judges, and a trial for that piece of human garbage? How old are the boys?"

"Adam, zhiz iz November 1917. Theodore juzt turned thirteen lazt month, and Allan turned eight back in May. Zhe boyz are five yearz apart."

"Oh, yea, I got it now, Annaliese. Their ages just sometimes slips my mind. Anyway, I thought to take you, the boys and that cat ... what is its name?"

"Figgy-vell. Zhe boyz named zee cat Figgy-vell. I zink it iz cute."

"Okay, alright. Figgy-well. That's a different name for a cat. Fine. Anyway, I thought all of us could head on over to Central Park and take in the holiday festive atmosphere of the city."

"Oh, Adam, it iz a bit too nippy outzide for me. Und I have much cookin' to do. You und zee boyz go 'head, enjoy yourselvez, be zafe on your way to zee park, und be zafe comin' home."

"Alright, Annaliese. C'mon boys, let's head over to Central Park and see what fish are in the pond. I'm not too crazy about watching that cat, so I'll leave it here with you, Annaliese."

"Zat iz fine, Adam. Vatch zee boyz clozely, Adam, pleeze."

"I will, Annaliese, I will."

\* \* \* \*

"Ahh, here we are fellas. Let's see if any fish are in there and ... Whoa! You startled me, Ma'am. Seeing your reflection in the pond over my shoulder gave me quite a start."

"I'm sorry. I didn't mean to frighten you nor the boys that are with you."

"Well, that's okay. At least I didn't fall over into the water. And you boys quit snickering. You probably wished I had of fell in. That would have given you a good laugh, right?"

"Yes, daddy, that would have been quite funny, wouldn't it Al?"

"Yea."

"You guys can quit laughing, cause I'm stayin' on dry land."

"My apologies, sir. I just enjoy being near the water and the surrounding grasses and trees. And the way you peered over into the water, I figured I'd come and see what you were looking at, which I hoped you wouldn't mind. You didn't, did you? You didn't mind me looking over your shoulder?"

"No, not at all. I was just surprised."

"Good. My name is Nereidia."

"Pleased to meet you, Nereidia. I'm Adam, and these are my two boys, Theodore and Allan. I figured I'd bring them out to the park, even though it is a bit nippy out here. My wife would've come, but she has too much cooking to do."

"Sounds like you have a lovely family, Adam. I can see that you and your boys are handsome fellas. I bet your wife is pretty, isn't she?"

"She is, at least to me she is very pretty. Her name is Annaliese."

"Ahh, it sounds German."

"Yes, she is from Germany. I think she, at times, wishes she could go back there to visit. But we've settled in fairly well over in Queens. How about you? Where do you live?"

"I live over on the New Jersey side of the Hudson River near the tributaries that flow into the Atlantic Ocean. Like I said, I enjoy, actually I really love, being near the water. Maybe that's because of my last name, which is Waters ... Nereidia Waters."

"That's pretty cool, Nereidia. I suppose if my last name related to what I love to do, it would be Horse ... Adam Horse."

"Alright, Adam ... ha, ha. Excuse me for chuckling. You're pretty funny. You must be around horses a lot?"

"I am. I do it for a living. I'm a trainer of thoroughbred race horses. Matter-of-fact, that is part of the reason why me and the boys are here at Central Park. I wanted to spend some time with them before I take off on the road in a few weeks to head upstate where I conduct much of the training. I got to get ready for the upcoming 1918 racing season, that is if this European war doesn't get in my way"

"I see, Adam. Where do you go in upstate New York to do your training?"

"Saratoga. That's where Mr. Wheelhouse, my boss, maintains his stables. He has established Saratoga as his home base."

"How exciting. I enjoy watching horses race. With all the color and parading the horses around, and the women in their big, fancy hats, it's all quite entertaining."

"You bet it is. My wife use to work in a hat shop making those fancy hats. Maybe you can come to Saratoga next year and take in some of the activities. We have several fine horses that, I believe, are potential derby winners. You ought to come and check us out, if you can."

"Yes, I will Adam Hart. You've talked me into it. I have to go now, but maybe we'll see each other again, and I can meet your wife. Goodbye."

"Goodbye, Nerdina. I hope to see you soon."

"It's Nereidia, Adam. Nereidia. You'll see me again. Take care."

"You take care too. Well, boys, what do you say we go get a bite to eat and then head on back home?"

"You know what dad?"

"No, what Theodore?"

"That lady was very pretty, but she didn't seem to mind the cold weather here in November. I mean, her dress was very skimpy-looking, and kind-of see through almost. I don't think she had on any underclothes. She must be used to the cold."

"Well, you know, Theodore, some people enjoy the cold weather. I guess it's refreshing to them. Maybe she feels it helps her to stay healthy. Some are like that, you know."

"Yea, I guess. Dad, I don't know if you noticed this, but I sure did.

"What you talkin' bout, Theodore? What did you notice?"

"She was barefoot!"

\* \* \* \*

My goodness, a pret-'y lady scan-'ily dressed and barefoot walkin' in New York City's Central Park in November! How weird is 'hat? Me thinks she's uh bi-differen' and ... uhh, sorry Guv-nuh, for me accen' I mean. I'll do bet-'er. Anyway, America is now fully helpin' us Brits in World War I. America's colored troops are in France, I hear, involved in heavy fightin' here in 1918. Also, anut-'her type of deadly fightin' is-uh goin' on in 1918 at home in New York direc-'ly affec-'in' Adam and Annaliese, and e're-body else in America too. You know wha't? It's uh virulent attack on duh world's population. For Adam, it starts at Saratoga.

* * * *

"Horace, bring that horse, Blueboy, over to the paddock. We'll run him some, give him a good workout and see what his time is before we race him Saturday."

"Yes, suh, Mr. Adam, right away, suh."

"Walk him around a bit, Horace, then saddle him up. You can ride 'em since you're a little light-weight guy. I just want to see how he ... oh, it's you, the lady from the park. You made it up."

"Yes, Adam, I made it. Like I said, I love to watch horses race."

"You know, today is not a race day. This is a training day. The races will begin in a couple of days. But tell me, how'd you get in here? We are not open to the public today. And what was your name?"

"It's Nereidia, Adam, Nereidia Waters. And apparently security did not mind me coming in. I had no trouble finding you."

"Well, uhm, Nereidia, you really shouldn't be here. We're in training."

"I, uh, I would just like to watch how you train a horse, Adam. How you evaluate the horse as he races by, his muscles flexing with those long, graceful strides of his legs. And then I want to see how you rub the horse down with your strong hands after he's through running with sweat pouring off his neck and back. How you massage his chest, legs, thighs and torso, and then give him a nice pat on his rump for good measure. All this is so, how shall I say, is so intriguing. Please allow me to stay, Adam. I won't get in your way, honest. I'll just stay over here by my lonesome self and simply observe. I'm always alone with no one to pat me down or caress my, uhh, chest or massage my torso and backside, or legs or rub me ... you know where. I'm just trying to say, Adam, that I'll keep to myself. Believe me, I will. Please allow me to stay, will you Adam?"

"Alright. I guess it's okay for you to watch. You certainly know how to lay on the charm. C'mon, walk with me over here to this observation area near the track. You'll be able to see everything, and you won't get in the way. My assistant, Horace, is getting ready to give one of our horses, Blueboy, a mild workout. I'll need to go over and talk to him."

"Thank you, Adam. Let me hold onto your arm, if you don't mind. I feel my feet kind of slipping on this wet ground. These new heels I'm wearing haven't been broken in yet, and I prefer to go bare-legged, you know ... no stockings, until I'm more comfortable in wearing these new heels. You don't mind, do you?"

No, I don't mind at all, Nereidia. I don't want you to fall either. Now you will have to wait right here while I go over and talk to Horace for a bit. There are certain elements of this horses' running style that I want to examine. You know, you might just be able to see a race today. Not an actual race for the money, but a training race to see how a horse runs against competition."

"That would be wonderful, Adam. I'd love to see that. I'll stand right here and watch and wait for you."

"Good. You'll see a lot from there. I'll be back. Horace! Horace! Let me talk to you for a minute ... come with me over here. I need to talk with you for a bit. And bring Blueboy over, let me see him. I want to take a close look at his legs and hooves."

"Sure, Mr. Adam, here we are. Somethin' botherin' you? Just havin' Blueboy walk and then trot a bit was fine. I didn't pick up on anythin' wrong. At least not yet, anyways."

"No, I'm not too concerned about Blueboy, Horace. He looks good. I am anxious to see how he'll run when you put him on the track. But you see that woman, her skin kind of a lightly tan olive complexion, way over there near the stable entrance? See her with that long brown hair down to her shoulders?"

"Oh, yes sir. I seen her soon as she came up by you. A very pretty thing too. That short dress and short light overcoat she's wearin' is showin' off her long, pretty legs. I mean, they goes from the ground and they reach all the way up to the sky and touch heaven. Glory be to God."

"Alright, alright, Horace, that's enough fawning and fantasizing over her."

"Oh, sorry Mr. Adam. Didn't mean to get carried away like that, sir."

"That's okay. She kind of worries me though, Horace."

"Sir, how's that, Mr. Adam? What do you mean she kind of worries you? How could you be worried over a beautiful creature like that?"

"Well, about a month or so ago, I first ran into her at Central Park in the City when I had my boys with me. It's like she just popped up out of nowhere. I mean, I was startled.

Anyway, we started talking and, after some nice conversation, I invited her to come up to Saratoga for the races."

"Well, Mr. Adam, there you have it. You invited her up and she's here."

"No, Horace, I invited her up to see the races since she said she likes to watch horses race. I did not expect her, nor did I want her, to come to our training sessions. There is something seductively odd about her."

"Sir, if I may so, Mr. Adam, the only odd thing I see off hand is how lightly she is dressed given this type of weather we're havin' right now. I mean, it was cloudy earlier, and we had a light drizzle of rain earlier this mornin' and it ain't exactly hot right now, but kinda still on the cool side to me. And now it's late mornin' near 'bout noon, maybe sixty degrees and yet she's dressed like it's eighty degrees out here."

"Yes, I noticed that too, Horace. Her dress doesn't quite fit the weather at the moment. I wonder if she's a spy from one of our competitor's stables, you know, like from the Hadley Ranch? They can be pretty slick, you know. I never cared much for any of them."

"Well, I don't know 'bout that, Mr. Adam. It seems like to me she's more interested in you than spyin' on any horse. I saw how she was holdin' onto your arm, and leanin' into your shoulder, like she was really close."

"Aw, man, that was nothing. She was afraid that she might slip and fall on the wet ground where we were. She had on some new heels. So, she was just holding onto my arm so she wouldn't lose her balance."

"Beg pardon, Mr. Adam, sir, that could be. But she didn't look like she was havin' any trouble when she first walked up to you. I tell you what though, sir."

"What's that, Horace?"

"When she turned a certain way durin' a sun break shinin' through the clouds, I swear I could see right through her light coat and dress like they was sheer. Mr. Adam, sir, I tell you, she does not have a stitch of underclothes on. I mean, no slip, no bra, no panties, no nothing. She is completely nude underneath that light bit of clothing. Honestly, Sir, it's clouded back up now, but I could tell when the sun was hittin' her."

"Horace, man, you make me laugh. I think your imagination is running away with you."

"Yes sir, Mr. Adam, sir. But as we say back home, that woman can show put lead in my pencil if I had someone to write too!"

"Alright, alright. That's enough jokes, Horace. Let's get busy and give this horse a good workout. I want Blueboy to be in tip-top shape for Saturday. If he doesn't win, he's got to come in no further back than third with a decent time to have a chance to run in the derby later this year. So, let's get him going, okay?"

"Yes, sir, right away Mr. Adam, sir. Oh, by the way, look over yonder there. Your lady friend is gone."

*  *  *  *

"Well, Mr. Adam, I believe we did the best we could to get Blueboy into top racing form to compete today on this warm Saturday afternoon."

"Yea, Horace, I agree with you. I just hope he can stay ahead of the field, run the type of race he's capable of running, and finish in the top three, preferably as the winner. Let me see that list of horses running in the race with Blueboy."

"Yes, sir. I'm not to good at readin', but I can tell you the names of the other horses, a little bit of their racin' tendencies, you know — what they likes to do, and the colors they run under."

"That's right, Horace, you do have a lock-down steel trap of a memory. Go ahead, tell me what you know. And let's not forget to tell the jockey Mr. Wheelhouse has chosen. I haven't learned who that is yet, but we'll find out shortly. Our usual boy, Johnny Reb, is out sick today, at least that is what I was told. So, tell me what you know about the competition in this race. I do know that our horse, Blueboy, will be in the first position next to the rail running under his blue banner. I just hope he can maintain his space and not get banged into the rail by some other horse. So, tell me about the others."

"Yes sir, Mr. Adam. In the number two position will be Red Dancer running under the red banner. He likes to get out fast."

"Umm, he'll be in the number two position which means he'll be next to our horse. Do you think he might veer to his left and bang into our horse?"

"No, sir, I don't think so, Mr. Adam. From what I hear, Red Dancer tends to run pretty straight and clear. But he will jump out to a fast start right from the starter's flag-drop signal."

"Alright, that sounds pretty good, Horace. Please, continue."

"Lé-mon, kind of French sounding, is in third position. He runs under the yellow colors. He's also a quick starter. In fourth position is Verdant. He tends to run sort of middle-of-the-road. Green is the color of his banners. Fifth position is held by Coral. He's a slow starter but can kick it near the end. Colors are orange. In position six is Whitewood running under the white banners. That horse tends to stay back and, like he's surveying the field to wait and see what the other horses are going to do, then he makes his move, usually down the back stretch."

"Goodness, Horace, you have all this committed to memory?"

"Well, Mr. Adam sir, I goes to a lot of horse races, and I've seen everyone of these horses in this field run, some more than once. I writes things down and then commits them to my memory."

"Goodness, I'm impressed. I knew you were a good horseman, but I didn't know you were that good. I mean, you are great, Horace! Is that it about the field in this next race?"

"No sir, one more, Negril. He's in the seventh and final position. His colors are black. Now this horse has a history of being frisky and fidgety at the start. If he cuts up too much, he could get scratched. I seen that happen to him about three months ago. But if he has a good start and runs well, watch out. That's the field, Mr. Adam, seven horses including our Blueboy."

"Okay, Horace. Great job. Go on over to that platform and call the race for me ... and some company it looks like I see coming over. Hello, Miss Waters, or is it Mrs. Waters?"

"Good afternoon, Adam. It's Miss, but please call me Nereidia. And a good afternoon to you to, Horace, if I heard your name said correctly."

"Afta-noon, Ma'am; and yes, you said my name right."

"Listen, Horace, I have to go find Mr. Wheelhouse and the new boy that's going to ride Blueboy today. I need to tell them what you just told me about the competition Blueboy will be facing. I'll have them come over here too. We still have plenty of time before the race begins, so I'll be right back. Maybe you can tell the lady here a thing or two about horse racing. Okay? Honestly, Near-ee-da, or however you say your name, I'll be back as soon as I can. You go ahead and talk to Horace here. I'll be back before you know it."

"Take your time, Adam. I'll enjoy talking with Horace, and hopefully he with me, won't you, Horace?"

"Yes, Ma'am. I, uhh, I'll do my best till Mr. Adam gets back."

"Well, Horace, tell me all about horse racing?"

"Uhh, Ma'am, I ... I don't rightly know if there's much to tell. The horses, they just run around this here track until they reach the finish line down there aways. Whoever crosses that finish line first is the winner. And dependin' upon the odds, the winner could pay off pretty big. That's 'bout it, Ma'am."

"That sounds marvelous, Horace, just marvelous. But I need you to tell me about something else I saw as I was coming over here."

"Oh, what is it you saw and where?"

"Come follow me, it's over here, behind this barn or I guess you call it a stable. But come, let me show you. It really has me puzzled. Come on, quickly, this won't take long."

"Aww-right, aww-right, but this has to be fast. The race our horse is in will be startin' pretty soon. So, real fast, show me what you talkin' 'bout. Hey, don't go too fast ahead of me.

I can't see you now that you've turned that corner. Let me catch up to you after I turn this corner, and ... Hey, where are you? Where'd you go? Ma'am? Ma'am? I'm going to turn around and head back to the platform if you don't show yourself. Are you playin' some kind of game or trick? Aww-right, I'm..."

"Please, turn around, Horace."

"Holy Jesus! Why are you naked? Where are your clothes? What ... what are you doing?"

"Look at my creamy white skin, Horace. Doesn't it appeal to you? And my breasts, see how my pink nipples sparkle. They sparkle for you, Horace."

"Jesus woman, you picked a bad time to come onto me right about now. I got to ..."

"Shhh, come here Horace. Here, place your hand on my breast. Feel how full and firm it is. Go ahead, hold it, squeeze it. The other one to. Yea, that's it. Let me show you what I can do for you, Horace. It won't take long. This will be really fast. I'll make you get off quickly. Let me show you how delightful I can be. And ... ummm ... Horace, you kiss so good! Here, let me have this."

"Jesus, miss whatever-your-name-is, you're makin' me ... oh God, oh God. That's good, honey, you, you makes me be feelin' so good ... oh God, oh God. Your head of hair feels so fine and soft. I'm going to ... oooo ... God help me. Sweet Jesus, I'm going to, I'm going to cu..."

\* \* \* \*

"Velcome home, Adam, my tall, dark, handzome huzband. Me und zee boyz mizzed you, und our cat, Figgy-vell, mizzed you. Our little Jamaica, Queenz neighborhood iz not zee zame vhen you are not here."

"Thank you, Annaliese. It's good seeing you too. Where are the boys?"

"Zay vent over to Central Park to play. By zhe vay, a lady came by, zaid zhe met you und zee boyz at zee park zum time ago. Adam, vhat iz zhe matter? Vhy you look zo zad? Your horze looze? Pretty badly?"

"No, Blueboy did not lose badly. He did fine, came in second behind a horse named Negril who just outran the entire field. He won by at least a length or two."

"Okay. Zo, vhy are your eyez all red ... und vet, like you been cryin'?"

"I have been crying, Annaliese. My assistant, Horace, was found dead behind one of the stables, apparently from a heart attack, says the doctor."

"Vhat? Oh, Adam, I'm zo zorry to hear zat. I am zo zorry."

"The doc also said Horace may have been developing the flu or pneumonia from what he could tell from the amount of sweat on his body. But there were no marks on him, and no signs of a struggle or foul play. It seems like his heart just gave out on him and he collapsed. The doctor said he doubt if Horace felt anything. He was likely dead before he hit the ground. I didn't even know he had a bad heart. It's very sad, Annaliese, very sad. I will miss him greatly."

"Come here, Adam, let me give you a varm hug. I am zo zorry for you. I know you und Horace vas very cloze. I truly am zo zorry."

"Ohh, thank you, baby. You feel good. But now, tell me about this lady you said came by to see me. I bet she was probably asking about me training a horse of hers, maybe?"

"Vell, zhe did mention zhe liked horzez und knew you vorked vith zhem. You und her had talked at zee park, apparently. Anyvay, zhe vas a very nice lady, vell-drezzed.

Zhe had on a beautiful, elegant hat zhat reminded me of our hatz at zhe millinery zhop. Zhe zaw you und zhe boyz come here to zee houze, zo zee vanted to ztop by und zay hello. Vee talked, und zhen zhe gave me a hug und left. Zat's it. Odd zhough. Figgy-vell did not like her. Zhe hissed at zee lady zeveral timez. I finally had to take her und put her outzide."

"I don't care so much about that cat, Annaliese. Did the lady leave her name?"

"Yez, zhe did. I cannot pronounze; it vas zumzing like Ner-i-da. I don't know, Adam, Ner-i-da iz zhe bezt I can zay. But, zuddenly I don't feel zo vell. I'm going to go lay down. Ve can talk later. I vant to azk you more about Ner-i-da."

* * * *

Well guv-nah, looks like Annaliese dun become sick, maybe af-'uh 'at visi't wi' 'he lady, Nereidia, hey? I wonder. Did Nereidia have somin' 'uh do wi' Horace's hear't uh-'ack?

Pardon me as I try 'uh shed 'is accen' I am. Strange woman, 'at Nereidia, if-'n she be a woman. Could be more of uh spook, yuh know. Muh fella feline sure didn' like her, naw't one bi't. Bu't life goes on ... righ'? Yea, sure does. And so, on we go for our nex' sor'ree."

*The Beautiful Bird - Egret*

# THE ASCENSION

 Uh year 1918 is fasci-'na-in. Pard'n me, guv-nuh, Shȳne hea. I'm goin' uh keep workin' on muh cockney accen' I am. Blimey, 'is bloody hard 'uh do. Buh em tryin' me best. Back tuh 1918, World War I is in full savage 'hrottle in Europe and involvin' America, Japan, Russia ... sor-'of, and whomever else was involved. Chlorine gas was cer'-inly involved released by 'hose bloody Jerrys, uh, I mean Germans, hi-'t our French allies. Un-'hen, mus-'ard gas. We hi-'t back and we hi-'t back hard with gas also. Ere'body ge-'n blis-'ers erey-where on 'hemselves ... eyes, skin, lungs, ere-'place. Many 'housands uh men killed on both sides. Ere-'body wearin' gas masks lookin' like aliens from Mars. An' wearin' clothin' for pro-'eck-shun from gas, buh nawt good agin' at 1918 plague outbreak ... a worldwide deadly rum-pudge uh Spanish Flu!

\* \* \* \*

"Good morning, Madame Lilly-Ann."

"Good morning, ladies. Please, take your seats. I truly do appreciate the respect you beautiful, wonderful women have shown me. Ignoring my mixed-race heritage and African American ethnicity, you have honored me by allowing me to oversee you and the management of our millinery shop while Madame Mitzi is ill suffering with this flu that's been going around. For your loyalty and willingness to follow my lead, I am deeply honored and grateful. I mean this from the bottom of my heart."

"Miss Lilly-Ann, may I say something?"

"Yes, Bërta, please, help yourself. The floor is yours."

"C'mon girls, all together, three cheers for our own great leader, Lilly-Ann. Here we go … Hip-hip, Hooray … Hip-hip, Hooray … Hip-hip, Hooray!"

"Thank you! I love each of you. Thank you so much. But now, ladies, we have work to do. Lots of orders here as usual. But I have a unique hat and dress order here I want to share with you. This was given to me by our own Coriander. I think this came from a cousin of hers. Is that right, Coriander?"

"Yes, Madame Lilly Ann, my cousin, Lucy, was in the great San Francisco earthquake, uhh, twelve years ago … is that right? It's been twelve years since that earthquake hit San Francisco? Let me see this is …"

"That's right, Coriander. It's been twelve years, 1906, since that devasting earthquake hit San Francisco."

"Good, I was hoping my arithmetic was right. Thank you, Madame Lilly Ann. Anyway, Lucy was ten at the time. Her mother, my aunt, was killed. Her dad took Lucy and her brother, James, and moved to Kansas. He didn't want any more exposure to earthquakes."

"Sounds like he moved right into tornado alley there, Coriander. But go ahead, sorry to interrupt."

"That's alright Madame Lilly Ann. Anyway, Lucy is now twenty-two, moved to Detroit, has a good job in one of the factory plants there, looking to get married, and is ready to make a statement in the world of high-fashion and dress. For starters, she wants a couple of very fancy hats. So, she reached out to me and here we are with her order. I believe that, over time, many more orders will follow, especially from her friends. There you go, Madame Lilly Ann. That's about it."

"Thank you, Coriander, great story. Now, ladies … uh, yes, Coriander, you want to say something else?"

"No, that's alright Madame Lilly Ann. I, uh, that was it, about my cousin, Lucy, I mean."

"You sure? I saw you raise your hand slightly, Coriander."

"No Ma'am, it's nothing. I'm fine. I've … I've said what I, uh, wanted to say. Thank you."

"Alright. Well, ladies, plenty of orders here. And before I give these out, I want to make note of several of them. A number of these orders are from the wives and girlfriends of our soldiers who were wounded while fighting in Europe against the Germans in this awful war. I sure hope this year of 1918 will see a blasted end to it.

Anyway, these women want to look real fancy and nice when their wounded men come home. So, let's put our best into it, as we always do. And let's remember our men that are still fighting over there. Oh, and let's remember Mitzi and Annaliese. I was down in New York City a few days ago to see Annaliese, and she is sick to, like Mitzi, with this flu that's going around. I want to make a couple nice hats for them. And ... that's about it ladies. Unless anybody has anything else, they would like to share? Anybody? Anyone? Last call. No one? Alright, let's get busy."

*  *  *  *

"Hello, my name is Lilly Ann. May I help you?"

"Yes, I sure hope so. I'm looking to have a couple custom-made hats developed for me. Actually though, they are for a couple friends I plan to give them as a gift. Both have been ill, and I thought a nice, fancy hat might cheer them up. And I understand your millinery shop has a fine reputation for making great looking hats for women."

"Thank you, we appreciate your confidence. And yes, by all means, we can certainly provide the type of hat you are looking for. We have some of the best millinery designers in the country. I am quite confident we can deliver what you are looking for."

"Excellent! I believe you can too. What do I need to do?"

"Great! Let me get a work order form for you to complete Miss, uh ... may I have your name?"

"Nereidia; Nereidia Waters."

"Oh, what a pretty name. Is there a meaning behind it?"

"Yes, my first name relates to my last name. Nereidia is associated with water, you know, one who identifies with water such as lakes, streams, rivers, the ocean, that sort of thing."

"Interesting! How do you spell your first name?"

"N-e-r-e-i-d-i-a; pronounced Neer-ĭd-dee-uh."

"Great! Thank you, Nereidia. What I need you to do is take this work order form and complete it with as much information and detail as you can. I've written in your name here. We will need your address, style of hat you want, type of decor, size dimensions, the occasion for its use, your desired completion date, and so on. It's a rather detailed form, so please, take it home with you. Complete it at your leisure and simply bring it back here to the shop when you're finished, and we'll get right to work on it. How does that sound?"

"That sounds fine, Lilly Ann. I should have this back to you within a few days, if not later today. Thank you, and I'll be back soon. Goodbye!"

"Goodbye, Nereidia. We look forward to seeing you again. Bye now, and you take care."

"That was an interesting looking customer, Madame Lilly Ann."

"Yes, Coriander, quite interesting. She was very elegantly dressed, wasn't she? Her name is Nereidia; Nereidia Waters. Kind of different, huh?"

"Yes, quite so. She was very beautiful, although it was kind of a strange or different-looking, foreign-like beauty about her ... almost haunting."

"Excuse me, Coriander. Madame Lilly Ann."

"Yes, Bërta."

"May I see you for a few minutes? I have some questions about a couple of these hat work orders I have."

"Sure, I'll be right there. Okay, Coriander, we can discuss our new customer later. I'd be curious to know what else you observed about Miss Nereidia."

"Okay, Madame Lilly Ann, that's fine with me."

"Good! Alright, Bërta, let's see the work orders you are concerned about."

"Yes, follow me, they're over here at my worktable. The paperwork is fully completed just fine. However, this customer is requesting a design that would involve the use of Egret feathers if not the actual bird itself. And that is something we can no longer do, right? I mean, it is still against the law to use birds or even just bird feathers in the creation of our hats, right? That hasn't changed has it, Madame Lilly Ann?"

"No, Bërta, that has not changed. Those bird and wildlife protection laws have been in place for at least a dozen years or more. I mean, that started under President Theodore Roosevelt for goodness sake. Who is the customer on these work orders? Here, let me take a look at them."

"Sure, here you go. The customer has an odd or at least a different name that I've never heard before. Here, you see, the customer's name is Nereidia ... Nereidia Waters. And I, uhh ... uhh ... Madame Lilly Ann! Madame Lilly Ann! Are you alright? Madame Lilly Ann! You okay? Did I say something wrong?"

"No, Bërta, you did not say anything wrong. It's just ... it's just impossible! How can this be? Oh God, I'm beginning to feel faint. I must sit down."

"Someone ... Coriander, please get a glass of water for Madame Lilly Ann. Hurry! She's not feeling well. Take it easy, Madame Lilly Ann. Coriander is bringing you some water."

"Thank you, Bërta. I'm kind of in a state of shock right now."

"Oh! Why is that? Was it something about these work orders I showed you?"

"Here you go, Madame Lilly Ann. Take a sip of this water and relax yourself. Maybe you need to go and lay down."

"Thank you, Coriander. I'll ... I'll be alright in a few minutes, I think. Coriander ... Coriander, t-t-take ... take a look at the name on Bërta's work orders. Bërta, please show them to her."

"Sure, alright. Here you go, Coriander."

"Okay, thanks Bërta. Let's see, her name, her name, let me locate her na ... What! Nereidia Waters? What ... What is this, some kind of hoax? How can this be? I ... I ... I ... don't believe it!

I just simply don't believe it! Nereidia Waters! It can't be! It simply can't possibly be!!!"

"Coriander, Coriander."

"Y-Y-Ye ... Yes, Madam Lilly Ann. I don't understand. I can't ... I can't..."

"Coriander, that is MY hand-writing of her name!"

\* \* \* \*

"Hi, boys. Kind of a nice October evening here in Central Park isn't it?"

"Uhh, yes Ma'am."

"Don't be frightened. You remember me don't you, from when I met you boys along with your father here in this park some time ago? You do remember me, don't you?"

"Yea, I 'member you, lady. You had an odd name."

"Yes, that's right, Theodore. It is Theodore isn't it? And you are Allan, right?"

"Yea, that's right. I'm Theodore and this here is my little brother, Allan."

"Right, and your father's name is Adam; and your mother is called Annaliese. Right?"

"That's right, Miss, uhh..."

"Nereidia. My name is Nereidia."

"Okay, thanks, uhhh, Neer-i-da."

"That's alright, Theodore, most people have a hard time saying my name. Say, I'd like to ask your mom and dad something. Are they at home?"

"Yea, at least mom is. C'mon!"

"Great! Thank you, Theodore. You boys getting ready to celebrate the new festival of All Saints' Eve?"

"The festival of what? I don't know what you're talkin' 'bout lady. We never heard of a festival of whatever you said. What'd you call it?"

"All Saints' Eve. It's an observance brought here by people from Europe. A time when spirits, sometimes not so friendly spirits, are about causing all kinds of mischief and trouble."

\* \* \* \*

"Hello! Oh, it iz you again, Mizz uhhh ... vhat vas your name?"

"Nereidia, Annaliese, my name is Nereidia Waters. We met, briefly, once before."

"Yez, I remember. I vould invite you in, but I haven't been feeling vell lately. Und vhatever I have, I don't vant to give it to you."

"Oh, I'm quite sure it won't affect me, Annaliese. I've developed a pretty strong immunity to this sort of thing. I won't take up much of your time. There are a number of other visits I need to make today, and some are located across the state. So, I won't be long. Besides, I recall that your cat did not like me very well."

"Yez, that iz right. Figgy-vell really put up a fuzz in your prezence, zumzing zat female cat doez not normally do. Very ztrange."

"Well, that's quite alright. Would you like for me to prepare you something to eat? I'm a pretty good cook, so my friends tell me. And I'm doing that for several others that have come down with this terrible flu. I even did some cooking for your fellow co-worker, Mitzi."

"No, no, zat's okay. I'm fine, and bezidez, I'm not very hungry; no appetite right now."

"Alright. Well, anyway, please tell Adam that I am so sorry on hearing about the loss of his assistant, Horace. I could see they were very close. Please extend to him my deepest sympathies."

"Yez, I vill tell him."

"Thank you, and … go ahead and shake my hand. I assure you that your illness will not bother me at all, Annaliese. Like I said, I have a very strong immune system."

"Okay, if you zay zo. But don't zay I didn't varn you."

"Warning received, Annaliese."

"Vell, zanks for coming by, und like I zaid, I'll tell … my goodnezz your handz are cold."

"Sorry about that. I'm afraid I had my hands in some very cold water just before coming here. A few things I was doing required the use of cold water. Anyway, you were saying…?"

"I vill tell Adam you came by und zhat you extend zympathiez to him over zuh lozzing of Horaze. Uh-kay?"

"Okay. Great! Thank you, Annaliese. Goodbye."

"Goot-bye. Oh, by zuh vay, if you zee my boyz out zhere, tell zem I zaid to come in."

"I will. So long."

"Goot-bye." And good riddance. My thoughtz tell me zumzing iz very ztrange about zat voman, und … cough-cough; cough-cough; cough-cough … zhere I go again vith zhis horrid coughing. I don't feel vell at all. I muzt go lay down. Maybe fix myzelf a hot toddy. I zink ve have zome honey, lemon und vhiskey around here zum-vhere. I'll make zuh water boiling hot und zee if all zat vill give me zum relief. God, I feelz terrible!"

\*\*\*\*

"Wow, Madame Lilly Ann, here we are ... you, me and Bërta here, the three of us enjoying a nice, lovely, fall afternoon lunch time at this beautiful park, and yet the presence of death seems to fill the air."

"Yes, Coriander, I agree. As we move toward the end of 1918, it doesn't seem like we're moving toward the end of this flu. To the contrary, it is developing into a full-blown epidemic that may get much worse before it gets better."

"Ladies, there's no doubt about it, this flu that's going around is going to get worse!"

"Oh, Bërta, you are saying that with such confidence. What makes you say that?"

"Well, Coriander, I read in the newspaper about how many of our soldiers fighting the Great War in Europe are getting sick, I mean deathly sick in some cases. Many of those sick soldiers will be coming home. When that happens, the flu-like symptoms affecting them will begin to spread here in New York and everywhere else."

"Good point, Bërta, very good point."

"Yes. Thank you, Madame Lilly Ann. I just hope and pray this flu illness going around does not last too long and kill too many of us."

"You know, Bërta, you just reminded me of something. I wonder if this flu affecting so many people has something to do with the disappearance of Rebecca? And maybe even her niece, Rachel too, for that matter." You know, it's a mystery about them both. What happened to them? None of us knows the answer to that question."

"You know, ladies, I joined the Millinery Shop kind of at the tail end of those strange activities. I never really quite fully understood what was going on or what had finally happened. Do either of you mind filling me in? That sure would at least satisfy my own curiosity, hopefully without killing me. You know as they say, curiosity killed the cat."

"Sure, Coriander. Bërta, let me do this since I was pretty much involved with this from the very beginning. I won't draw this out too long, Coriander. I don't want to make you bored or put you to sleep. Okay?"

"Okay, Madame Lilly Ann, that's fine. I am eager, though, to hear the complete story, at least as much as you can or are willing to tell me."

"Oh, that's no problem, Coriander. I'll tell you what I can remember. Rebecca first came to me with a weird story about some dreams her niece was having, and those dreams were about…"

\* \* \* \*

"Good morning, Madame Lilly Ann."

"Good morning, ladies. Please, take your seats. I have some very sad news for you today. Last night, our own Mitzi Schneider finally succumbed to this dreadful flu virus that started last year and is still raging around the country here in 1919. She put up a valiant fight, but it just wasn't enough. Please remember her parents and siblings in your thoughts and prayers. As soon as I hear about the funeral arrangements, I will let you know."

"Madame, Lilly Ann?"

"Yes, Bërta."

"Did she suffer much? I mean, I've been reading in the newspapers where this flu thing has spread all over the country, and really even around the world. Some places, like New York City, seem to get hit much worse than small towns like where we are here in Schuylerville."

"Yes, that's true, Bërta. You know, this flu bug is extremely contagious. Anyplace where you have a greater concentration of people, like in the big cities such as New York, there will be a much greater chance for the flu virus to spread affecting many, many more people. In regard to Mitzi, she did suffer, as you might can imagine. This flu, I think it's called the Spanish Flu, gets in your lungs and passageways making it increasingly difficult for one to breathe. When I was able to visit Mitzi, she complained how sore she was all over her body. It just ached. She ran fevers and did a lot of heavy coughing.

Eventually, it got to the point where her breathing became increasingly labored until last night she just couldn't breathe anymore, and she died. At least now she is at peace. Maybe she is finally spending time with that Negro guy she told us about who died in the train wreck she was involved in there in Paris several years ago. I remember she said it was the best romance she never had. Well, maybe now she is ... she is, forgive me for tearing up here ladies ... maybe now she is finally experiencing that heavenly best romance. Yes, Bërta, you want to say something?"

"Yes, I do. I'll stand if you don't mind. You know, Madame Lilly Ann, and to the rest of you ladies, Mitzi was so good at making hats for women to wear. I mean, she really had a creative gift for it. Before birds were banned for us to use in our hat-making work, I could see her taking the feathers of an Egret and putting together a hat with such exquisite design and workmanship, it made me want to buy a hat from her."

"Yes, ha ... ha ... ha ... Bërta, I have to chuckle on that one. But you are so right. She was gifted."

"Yes, she was. Let me say one more ... oh God, hold it together here Bërta ... let me just say one more thing. I believe Mitzi is now soaring into the heavens like an Egret ... her beautiful white wings spread wide and catches the wind; her glistening black feet, like an arrow, pointed straight back to help her glide; and her orange beak extending far out into a sharp point to pierce through the sky and the heavens, and ascend into eternity. That's what I see, and I am so glad she is in a better place free from all the pain and suffering she had to endure.

Wings ablaze—fly, Mitzi, fly."

\* \* \* \*

"I'd like to welcome all of you to this brief grave site memorial honoring the good life of our fellow co-worker and dear friend, Mitzi Schneider, who was taken from us all too soon. To all of you and on behalf of Mitzi's family, thank you for coming. This observance will be brief."

"I miss her so much already, Madam Lily Ann, I do."

"Yes, Bërta, she is so greatly missed. And let me say to all of you, Mitzi was not a religious person in the traditional sense of the word. But she did govern her life by a key religious principle ... that being to love thy neighbor as thyself. One would be hard pressed to find a person more dedicated than Mitzi in living that principle out in their daily life.

Whatever you needed, if she could provide it, she would. And if she couldn't provide what you needed, she would find somebody who could. It did not matter your status in life, how much money you had or didn't have, your race or your background, it simply did not matter. She loved everyone. We do not have the time or space to let everyone say something. But I do want to give a brief space of time to Bërta for her to give that beautiful tribute to Mitzi that she delivered at our shop. Bërta."

"Thank you, Madam Lily Ann. To the family, fellow co-workers, and friends, now that Mitzi is gone from us, and is released from all pain and suffering, I liken her present state as a beautiful, flying Egret bird that is soaring into the heavens. Her long, white, feathery wings are spread fully wide catching that seemingly ethereal endless wind that eventually will blow upon all of us, and that wind has carried her into eternity. God bless and receive you, Mitzi. Thank you for this space and time, Madam Lily Ann."

"Very beautifully said, Bërta. Thank you so much. I will close with a short chorus of an old Negro spiritual that I feel is appropriate to sing at this moment in time. Very briefly ...

♪ *Swing low, sweet chariot,*
*Comin' for to carry me home;*
*Swing low, sweet chariot,*
*Comin' for to carry me home. (x 2)*

*I looked over Jordan an' what did I see;*
*Comin' for to carry me home;*
*A band of angels comin' afta me;*
*Comin' for to carry me home.*

*Swing low, sweet chariot,*
*Comin' for to carry me home;*
*Swing low, sweet chariot,*
*Comin' for to carry me home.*

*If you get there befo' I do;*
*Comin' for to carry me home;*

*Tell all my friends I'm comin' too;*
*Comin' for to carry me home.*

*Swing low, sweet chariot,*
*Comin' for to carry me home;*
*Swing low, sweet chariot,*
*Comin' for to carry me home.*

"You know, there is an underlying meaning to the words of that tune used during Harriet Tubman's time to help my people escape from the evil clutches of slavery. And now Mitzi has escaped from the clutches of the pain and suffering that gripped her body since she contracted this deadly flu virus. Rest in peace my dear friend, Mitzi. Rest in peace ... Once again, I want to thank you all for coming. I'm sure Mitzi, looking down from above, is very pleased. This concludes our memorial. You may place your flowers on the casket before it is lowered into the ground. And travel safely as you make your way home. Thank you."

* * * *

"Happy New Year, Annaliese! 1920 is finally here. Are you feeling some better with the arrival of the new year?"

"I'm hangin' in zhere, Adam. But I'm very tired, Adam, very tired, und zore all over my body, just everyvhere."

"Well, the doctor says you have this flu that's been goin' around. I mean, it's been all over the city, around the state, and from what I've been hearin', it's been catchin' all around the entire country, and even the world. But it seems to be on the decline now."

"Zat may be, Adam, but not for me. I believe zat, Adam. I believe it iz been zpread 'round here by a flu carrier like your friend, zat lady, Neer-ida."

"Nereidia? Why her, Annaliese?"

"Zhe ... cough – cough – cough ... came here lazt year, tryin' to be friendly und all, vantin' to cook for me vhile I'm zick. Zhe zaid zhe vas doin' zat for otherz who vere zick. Neighborz, I guess, zat are around here und in uh-zher partz of zhe zity. Und, Mitzi, zhe zaid zhe visit Mitzi, right?"

"Yea, that's what I heard from some of your friends at the millinery shop when I was up at the track and I ran into them during one of the races. But, what of it? That don't mean nuthin'."

"Oh mein Gott, öffne die augen dieses blinden. Open your blind eyez, Adam, and zee vhat I zee. Sie sind alle tot, alle, die sie besucht hat. Zay are all dead, Adam, every-vone zhe visited ... Mitzi, neighborz, all gone. Und me? Very zoon, Adam my love, very zoon."

"You don't know that, Annaliese, you don't know that. I mean, you are letting your imagination run away with you. You always did have a big imagination. I can remember ..."

"Nein! Hör auf, Adam. Bitte geh jetzt, ich bin sehr müde, sehr müde. Please go, Adam. I am very tired, zo very tired."

"Alright, dear, you rest. I will go see the doctor tomorrow and ask what else we can do for you. There must be something else we can do. I love you, Annaliese. I love you so very much."

\* \* \* \*

"It's all my fault, Dad. I should not have brought that lady into see mother. I feel so bad now that ... now that she's gone."

"Theodore don't blame yourself. These things just happen. Some people recover from this, what do they call it, the, uh, Spanish Flu, and some don't. That's just the way it is. This time, the flu outbreak was everywhere. I read where thousands have died, and not just here in the United States, but in other countries too, like England and France."

"Yea, I know. But for mother to get it here, in her own house, and then die! No, it's my fault. I should have never let that Neer-ida woman in last year. I just shouldn't have. Anyway, I'm goin' out. Move out the way, Al, let me get through the front door. I'll see you all later."

"Alright, son, don't be too hard on yourself; and don't slam ... Bang! ... the door."

"Let me think, damn, I should not have let her in, I just should not have let her in and ... Oh, excuse me. I didn't see you there."

"That's okay. Your head was turned looking behind you as you were walking forward. Anyway, is Adam here? My name is Lily Ann from the hat shop where your mother use to work."

"Yea, he's in there. Go right up, knock on the door. Hey Dad! He may not can hear me with the door closed. Someone out here to see you! I have to go. By ma'am."

"Goodbye."

"Lily Ann! It's nice to see you. Come on in and have a seat."

"Hello, Adam. I wanted to come by and pay my respects to and your family over the passing of Annaliese. We really miss her, Mitzi, and the others. So many are dying from this flu epidemic. I'll be glad when it passes on."

"Me too, Lily Ann. But you seem to be holding up quite well."

"Yes, and so do you, Adam. I guess it's in our genes. Your boys appear to be doing well too, as are my kids."

"Yea. You know, Lily Ann, I went down to Central Park a few days ago after Annaliese died to just think and remember about our times together. And I saw something rather odd."

"Oh, what was that?"

"I was near the water, when all of these big, beautiful birds suddenly appeared on the water's edge. It must have been at least a dozen of them, maybe more. Just before they took off to fly away, that woman, Nereidia, appeared, barefoot and naked. Not a stitch of clothes on her anywhere except she wore a lady's hat, like the kind from your shop. She looked at me, turned her back toward me and began walking away toward a group of trees by the water's edge, and then ... poof, she just disappeared, so it seemed to me, into thin air. Then all those birds ... big, white, feathery birds ... took off all at once like some huge, great airplane, and soared into the sky. I mean, it was really something to see."

"Sounds like those birds were probably egrets, Adam."

"What makes you say that?"

"Oh, just a hunch. Hey, let's go grab a bite to eat. It's on me. And I'll buy us a bottle of wine to celebrate."

"To celebrate what, Lily Ann?"

"Life! C'mon, let's go. Besides, there is something else I want to tell you."

"Alright, Lilly Ann. We can walk to this little Italian place down the street here. It's only about three or four blocks away. They serve good food and good wine. We can talk on the way."

"Great! Adam, I haven't shared this with anyone yet, certainly no one at the millinery shop, but I plan to move back to New Orleans within the next year or two. I've had my fill of New York, and now that my kids are getting older, I think the South will provide a better environment for raising them when compared to the fast pace and trouble they could get into up here."

"You don't think your kids can get into trouble in New Orleans, Lilly Ann?"

"Oh, most certainly they can. But there is more of my family down there that can help them stay straight. You know, that southern upbringing."

"Okay. What about the hat shop? You just going to walk away from there?"

"Oh, they'll manage just fine. There are a lot of capable women there, any one of them could run the place quite well. They won't miss a beat. But there is something else, Adam"

"Okay. Well, here we are at the restaurant. Let's go inside and then you can tell me what that 'something else' is."

"Yes, for sure, I will."

"Is this table okay, Lilly Ann?"

"Yes, this is fine. Thank you, Adam. And I'll take whatever their house recommended red wine is."

"So will I. Now, tell me, Lilly Ann, what's on your mind?"

"I don't know if you know this, Adam, but we have a great horse racetrack in New Orleans called The Fair Grounds. It's been around since the mid-1800's."

"Oh, sure, Lilly Ann. I've been there a few times. You know, horse racing is my business and I go all over the country, even down into South America evaluating horses. Why do you ask?"

"Well, now that Annaliese has passed away and your boys are getting older where they can take care of themselves, I thought maybe you could come visit me sometime and check out the latest horses at the racetrack.

You could give me back that cat I gave to Annaliese and ... hey, don't choke on your wine there, Adam."

"I won't. You have just caught me by complete surprise talking like this, Lilly Ann."

"Well, I guess you might say I'm offering you a surprise gift, Adam. But you will have to unwrap it to see what it is."

* * * *

# CHEERS

"Well, ladies, I hope you did not do too much celebrating and drinking over this November 1924 election win of President Calvin Coolidge. I mean, you know we have to save some cheerful drinking for the holidays that are just around the corner. But listen to me, Miss Bashful Coriander, who am I to promote drinking since I don't do much of it myself. And you ladies can stop that giggling and ... Oh, I see her. She's coming up the walkway toward the millinery shop. You girls know the routine, we've been doing it for years now. It's a tradition. We stand and greet her in unison as soon as she come through the door. Alright, altogether now...

Good Morning, Madame Bërta."

"Good morning ladies. Please take your seats. I have some very good news for you today. Since we recently concluded the presidential election, and Mr. Coolidge has won, I have here a ton of work orders for our hats and dresses ... enough to keep this millinery shop in business for a very, very long time!"

* * * *

Hey, guv-nah, looks like 'em two, Lily Ann und Adam, may ge-'a-bi't squiffy i'-duz. May we should have uh tipple, uh glass uv a grea't-as'in port imported from Portugal, hey. Sure, why no't ... so 'ears tuh you, dea' reada' ladies ♀ an' gents ♂ —cheers!

Umm, a't-was good. Don' drink tuh much wine, howeva ' Read 'his poem eh foun' lyin' on 'nuh floor, I did. I'm a bi-'t 'ipsy meself, I am. 'Ear, read 'his.

* * * *

133

David Charles Hart

# AN ALCOHOLIC'S POEM

*I gazed long upon the glass, full of mixed drink.*

*Sparkling light crystal, smooth as long mink.*

*It glides down the palate, soothing as it goes.*

*Then bites like a viper, the beginning of many woes.*

*It stings like a bee ~ Strange things I then see.*

*Sprawled on the ground, groveling in the dirt.*

*They hit me and hit me. But I was not hurt.*

*They beat me and beat me. I felt nothing; I think.*

*When I wake up, I will look for more drink.*

\* \* \* \*

Eh, don-'t be like 'tha-'t fella, poor bloke.
    Sorry bou't Annaliese passin' away und all, und 'he uh-'hers also. Very sad. Bu' dyin be sum-'in we all have tuh reckon wi' sum-day. Righ't?
    However, life goes on it' duz. Und so, on tuh our nex'sor'ree. 'Ears good readin' tuh ya, guv-nah.
    Oh-oh, me see now 'his is the end, guv-nah.
    Well, I'm uh poor me ano-'her glass uv 'at port. As you can see, I'm uh peculiar grimalkin, I am.
    I can pour drinks und enjoy 'em wi' yuh. So, 'ears tuh you ... bo't-'ums up und ... Cheers!

# IMAGE REFERENCES

"Author Unknown;" File Name: Mode. Hattar. Modeplansch från 1911. PD-US; **Book Cover Picture.** This work is in the public domain because it originated before 1924; There are no known restrictions for its use under current copy right law. https://commons.wikimedia.org/wiki/File:NMA.0033994_Mode._Hattar._Modeplansch_fr%C3%A5n_1911.jpg

"Author Unknown;" File Name: Louis and Louisa Gregory; photo used for "**Long Live Queen Soteria;**" taken prior to 1924, circa 1911 – 1912. https://commons.wikimedia.org/wiki/File:Louis-and-Louisa-Gregory.png date accessed-May 7, 2019. Public Domain.

"Author Unknown;" File Name: Pixabay; Image of flying bird used for **The Ascension**; License is free for commercial use; No attribution required. https://pixabay.com/photos/animal-sky-bird-wild-birds-heron-3728905/

Barbosa, Dario Villares; File Name: Study of Female Nude-Google Art Project; painting, circa 1905, used for ... **Distortions**. https://en.wikipedia.org/wiki/File:Dario_Villares_Barbosa_-_Study_of_Female_Nude_-_Google_Art_Project.jpg date accessed-May 7. 2019. Public Domain.

Barribal, William H. (1873 - 1956); File Name: **Bluebird Lady**; created May 2, 1914; Library of Congress. Used for Cheers. Public Domain. https://www.loc.gov/pictures/item/2011649784/ last accessed Aug 30, 2019.

Maggs, Michael: Self-Commons user; File Name: Acer cappadocicum spring; photo-April 21, 2007-used for "**The Face In The Leaves**." https://commons.wikimedia.org/wiki/File:Acer_cappadocicum_spring.jpg#filelinks date accessed-May 7, 2019. Licensed under the Creative Commons Attribution-Share Alike 2.5 Generic arrangement and is free to be copied, distributed and transmitted. No alterations or changes made to image.

Moreau, Mathurin; File Name: Fluvial Nymph, (French, 1822–1912); **The Nereid Nymph.** From a fountain on the Place du Théâtre-Français, near the Rue de Richelieu, in Paris. Bronze, 1874. This image is in the public domain; last accessed Aug 30, 2019;
https://commons.wikimedia.org/wiki/File:Fluvial_nymph_Mathurin_Moreau.jpg

Paolo Neo, author; File Name: Red wine in glass in restaurant; This file is in the public domain, not copyrighted, no rights reserved, free for any use.
http://www.public-domain-image.com/full-image/food-and-drink-public-domain-images-pictures/wine-public-domain-images-pictures/red-wine-in-glass-in-restaurant.jpg.html

Sherman, Paul-WPClipart; File Name: Musical Box, photo-date taken is unknown; image used for "**The Music Box**"
https://www.wpclipart.com/music/listen/Musical_Box.png.html date accessed-May 7, 2019. Public Domain.

Studio Levy & Fils' Train Wreck at Montparnasse 1895; Paris, France, photo-October 22, 1895-used for "**The Best Romance I Never Had.**"
https://commons.wikimedia.org/wiki/File:Train_wreck_at_Montparnasse_1895.png date accessed-May 7, 2019. Public Domain.

CPSIA information can be obtained
at www.ICGtesting.com
Printed in the USA
FSHW011058101219
64878FS